W9-BNK-502

ADAM'S RETURN

Also by Richard Rohr

Everything Belongs, 1999, revised and updated edition, 2003

Called, Formed, Sent, with Thomas C. Welch, 2002

The Enneagram: A Christian Perspective, with Andreas Ebert, 2001

Hope Against Darkness: The Transforming Vision of St. Francis of Assisi in an Age of Anxiety, with John Bookser Feister, 2001

The Good News According to Luke: Spiritual Reflections, 1997

Jesus' Plan for a New World: The Sermon on the Mount, with John Bookser Feister, 1996

Job and the Mystery of Suffering: Spiritual Reflections, 1996

Enneagram II: Advancing Spiritual Discernment, 1995

Radical Grace: Daily Meditations, 1995

Quest for the Grail, 1994

Near Occasions of Grace, 1993

Experiencing the Enneagram, with Andreas Ebert et al., 1992

The Wild Man's Journey: Reflections on Male Spirituality, revised edition (with Joseph Martos), 1992, 1996

Simplicity: The Art of Living, 1991

Discovering the Enneagram: An Ancient Tool for a New Spiritual Journey, with Andreas Ebert, 1990

Why Be Catholic? Understanding our Experience and Tradition, with Joseph Martos, 1989

The Great Themes of Scripture: New Testament, with Joseph Martos, 1988

The Great Themes of Scripture: Old Testament, with Joseph Martos, 1987

ADAM'S RETURN

The Five Promises
of Male Initiation

RICHARD ROHR

INTERIOR ILLUSTRATIONS BY
JULIE LONNEMAN

A Crossroad Book
The Crossroad Publishing Company
New York

"Vacillation," by William Butler Yeats, is reprinted with the permission of Scribner, an imprint of Simon & Schuster Adult Publishing Group, from *The Collected Works of W. B. Yeats*, vol. 1: *The Poems, Revised*, edited by Richard J. Finneran. Copyright © 1933 by The Macmillan Company; copyright renewed ©1961 by Bertha Georgie Yeats.

"For the Time Being," copyright 1944 and renewed 1972 by W. H. Auden, from *Collected Poems* by W. H. Auden. Used by permission of Random House, Inc.

"Healing" by D. H. Lawrence from *The Complete Poems of D. H. Lawrence*, edited by V. de Sola Pinto and F. W. Roberts, copyright © 1964, 1971 by Angelo Ravagli and C. M. Weekley, Executors of the Estate of Frieda Lawrence Ravagli. Used by permission of Viking Penguin, a division of Penguin Group (USA) Inc.

The Crossroad Publishing Company
16 Penn Plaza, 481 Eighth Avenue
New York, NY 10001

Copyright © 2004 by Richard Rohr

All rights reserved. No part of this book may be reproduced, stored in a retrieval system, or transmitted, in any form or by any means, electronic, mechanical, photocopying, recording, or otherwise, without the written permission of The Crossroad Publishing Company.

This book is typeset in 12/16 Stone Informal. The display type is Tiepolo.

Printed in the United States of America

Library of Congress Cataloging-in-Publication Data

Rohr, Richard.
    Adam's return : the five promises of male initiation / Richard Rohr.
      p. cm.
    Includes bibliographical references.
    ISBN 0-8245-2280-X (alk. paper)
    1. Men–Religious life. 2. Spiritual life–Christianity. I. Title.
BV4440.R64 2004
248.2–dc22
                                  2004014956

2   3   4   5   6   7   8   9   10   10 09 08 07 06 05

Adamah, the first human name, means "of the earth."

For all the sons of Adam:

For those who are ashamed of being earth,
For those who love being earth too much,
For those who possess none of the earth,
For those who possess too much of it,

For those who need to know they are earth,
And try to flee to heaven out of shame,
Doubting the garden that they already have,
Abandoning the garden that they already are,

I dedicate this map of return.

CONTENTS

A WORD
FROM RICHARD

I WOULD LIKE YOU to know a bit about my background at the very beginning. Perhaps it will help you appreciate why I wrote this book. My educational background is in philosophy and theology, and I am self-educated in psychology and sacred story. I am a believing Catholic Christian, a Franciscan by spiritual choice, a spiritual director and community guide by experience, a teacher by gift, and a quasi hermit by preference. I read scholars but am not myself a scholar.

I am a synthesizer of sorts. My task is to get good news to the masses, not making it an elite or academic exercise for an in group. As St. Gregory of Nyssa (335–395) described his own job, mine is to "chew on" the appropriate texts and make them "delectable." This book is the result of having chewed on plenty of initiation texts, ancient and new, over a period of fifteen years, and I hope the reader will find the result both tasty and nourishing.[1]

This book is written by a white, middle-class American, who is secure, overeducated, ordained, unmarried, and male. Men like me are much of the structural and spiritual problem. We are sitting comfortably at the supposed top of the pile. And yet that truth, more than anything else, is why I *must* write this book. Men like me, with access to all manner of privilege and freedom not granted to others, must talk about the male game from within. I think you can unlock spiritual things only from within. Paralleling what women are saying about themselves, *men must first and finally interpret men.* Surely for the last twenty years, and maybe for much of history, we have largely been interpreted by whatever power group was in charge—doing none of us much good—and very recently by women, which has been both good and bad for us. Men have not, however, described their own souls very well, as if they did not have the language or even the interest. The oral tradition of the quest for the Holy Grail was probably our last serious attempt.[2]

Traditional initiation rites did just the opposite; they interpreted ordinary men from within—crediting maleness with its own innate spirituality — and worked at bringing men to wholeness from the bottom up, and from the inside out. I will try to do the same here, in the face of a culture, and a church, that usually tries to interpret men from the top down and from the outside in. Such a technique will never work, in my opinion, and it has not been working for some time. Our religious institutions are not giving very many men access to credible encounters with the Holy or even with their own wholeness. We largely give men mandates, scaffolding, signposts, and appealing images that tend to create religious identity and boundaries from the outside. But true happiness, like true enlightenment, is always an inside job. We will finally have to rely upon our own experience anyway, so we might as well guide men toward authentic religious experience. This is the true meaning of tradition, I think.

Though I am not a cultural anthropologist, nor an ethnologist, nor a sacramental theologian, I have talked to some experts, read everything I could,[3] and given men's retreats and male initiation rites for the past twenty years. I have traveled a great deal in doing so, giving conferences for men in North, South, and Central America, Eastern and Western Europe, and several parts of Asia, Africa, and Australia, and talked firsthand to formally initiated men in several cultures. My education on this subject has been largely in the field and on site, including fifteen years as a pastor of a lay community in Cincinnati and fifteen years as an Albuquerque county jail chaplain. All of which has told me who should be listened to and what is worth reading. I hope that puts this theory in touch with some kind of concrete practice. Let's call it "theology from below," which for me is the very meaning of the Incarnation and the descent of the Holy Spirit.

My continuing momentum in this work has been a rather constant sadness and disappointment over the lack of an inner life in so many men I meet, even among ministers, religious, and devoted laymen, and high-level and successful leaders from whom we would expect more. It is not their fault, if fault must be named. Usually no one has offered them anything more than Jacob's cheap "soup." We are sons of Esau, having sold our birthright for fast-food religion (Genesis 25:29–34). It does not deeply transform the self or the world.

So here are my viewpoints — remembering that every viewpoint is a view from a point, and all we can do is own them and bring them to consciousness: First, I believe that *truth is more likely to be found at the bottom and the edges of things than at the top or the center.* The top or center always has too much to prove and too much to protect. I learned this by connecting the dots of the Judeo-Christian Scriptures, from my Franciscan background — the pedagogy of the oppressed and the continued testimony of the saints and mystics — and from the first step of Alcoholics Anonymous. Final authority in the spiritual world does not tend to come from any agenda of success but from some form of suffering that always feels like the bottom. Insecurity and impermanence are the best spiritual teachers, as Alan Watts[4] and so many others demonstrate. The good news is clearly not a winner's script, although the ego and even the churches continually try to make it so.

Second, as Einstein put it, I believe that "no problem can be solved from the same level of consciousness that created it."[5] I try to teach a contemplative stance toward life that gives people an entirely new way of knowing the world, and that has the power to move them beyond mere ideology and dualistic thinking.[6] Frankly, what religion calls contemplation is the only mind that is broad enough and deep enough to answer the real and important questions. Mature religion will always lead you to some form of prayer, meditation, or contemplative mind to balance out our usually calculative mind. Such "seeing" — and that is what it is — always gives you the capacity to be happy and happily alone, rooted elsewhere, comfortable with paradox and mystery, and largely immune to mass consciousness and its false promises. It is called "wisdom seeing."

Third, I believe that I locate my thought somewhere between the social constructionist position (which says that the male psyche and identity are entirely formed by training and culture) and the essentialist position (which says that there is something inherent that comes with the male psyche and male biology). Outside this endless either/or argument, I believe that we are approximately one-third nature, one-third nurture, and one-third free choice. Such an opinion will probably please no one, but it is very important to me that we retain a strong notion of free will and the human dignity that goes with it, along with a recognition of both foundational male genes and later human conditioning. Otherwise, we end up with either a victim culture or a blame culture like we have in America today. We do not choose what happens to us, but we can cooperate with grace and choose our response to it (Romans 8:28).

I do not presume that there is some ideal masculinity floating around in Plato's cosmos, but there are, in fact, many masculinities. I hope I can make some contribution to gender studies here by honoring and empowering as many of these masculinities as possible. As a Franciscan Scotist by philosophical training, I believe that God creates only individuals, and God does not merely create genus or species, or what were called "universals."[7] Such a view should help us avoid any rigid ideology or big overarching explanation for everything, for in the end one must deal with *this* man in *this* moment and *this* place. I believe that is exactly what God does, and it is one of the most denied yet foundational themes of the Judeo-Christian Scriptures.[8] Such "election" or "chosenness" leaves grace and space around the edges of everything, and I hope we can do the same in this book.

Finally, I believe that our images and words for God matter deeply in the way we live our practical lives because we all become the God we worship. This has been a central breakthrough in awareness in recent decades, thanks largely to feminist theologians.[9] I believe that God is the ultimate combination of whatever it means to be male and whatever it means to be female. God is fully sexual in the deepest meaning of that term.[10] It is obvious to me that we must, therefore, find public ways to recognize, honor, and name the feminine nature of God, since we have overly limited our metaphors for God for centuries.

I will not eliminate or disallow all those wonderful sexually charged words for God — such as Mother, Father, Son, Daughter, Bride, Bridegroom, Friend, Guest, Lover, Jealous Lover, or even Seducer. Even more, I am not willing to eliminate the notion of God, a relationship with God, or the very word "God" (even though I know that every name for God, including the word itself, will always be a very limited metaphor and will carry a lot of baggage). I hope we can inaugurate a new humility in our use of religious language, which for me is the very proof that it is authentic. The Holy Mystery, our Higher Power if you will, is where all the power for ecstasy, endurance, love, and long-term transformation resides, and we dare not water initiation down to a superficial secularism. A true God always liberates us, primarily from ourselves and for something bigger. In that deep sense, God does save us, precisely by giving himself/herself to us and drawing us into the greater story.[11]

One

INITIATED INTO WHAT?

*Now that I have gone through my initiation,
I am ready for anything anywhere.*
— PAUL'S LETTER TO THE PHILIPPIANS, 4:12

*We do not have to risk the adventure alone;
for the heroes of all time have gone before
us. The labyrinth is thoroughly known; we
have only to follow the thread of the hero-
path. And where we had thought to find an
abomination, we shall find a god. Where we
had thought to slay another, we shall slay
ourselves. Where we had thought to travel
outward, we shall come to the center of our
own existence. Where we had thought to be
alone, we shall be with all the world.*
— JOSEPH CAMPBELL,
HERO WITH A THOUSAND FACES

HOW DO WE EXPLAIN the larger-than-life people we
occasionally meet in every country, in most institutions, even the smallest churches, and hidden away in
our neighborhoods? There always seem to be one or two
people who hold the energy of a group together, strategic
individuals whom the Bible would call "chosen people,"
men and women who move events and history forward,
sometimes almost invisibly. Where do such folks come
from? I have given up thinking that such people come
from any one religion, any one school of thought, any

1

particular race or nation, any specific socioeconomic sec-
tor, or even, indeed, that they are always perfect or moral
in the conventional sense. Spiritually powerful individuals seem to cross and defy all of these boundaries.

Something else seems to have happened to them, and
one way to put it is that they have somehow been "initiated." Initiated into their true self, initiated into the flow
of reality, initiated into the great patterns that are always
true, initiated into the life of God—choose the description
with which you are most comfortable. Such initiations
took specific ritual forms in every age and every continent
for most of human history. They were considered central
to the social survival of nearly every culture—and to the
spiritual survival of males in particular.

Patterns of initiation are the oldest system of spiritual
instruction that we know of, predating all institutional
religions. They emerged rather universally in what Karl
Jaspers calls Pre-Axial Consciousness, before the Axial
Age (800–200 BCE) when we began to organize thought
all over the world.[12] There is much evidence that this
Axial age has run its course and is now turning in on
itself. We see it in the bad effects of rationalism, individ-
ualism, and patriarchy. I believe this is at the heart of
many of our cultural and religious problems today. We
now need to recapitulate the wisdom of the pre-Axial
Age, together with the clarity and radiance of the Axial
Age. I will be taking just such a both-and approach in this
book, hopefully being fair to both ages and contributions.
Jaspers would call this II Axial Consciousness. I would just
call it the effects of the Spirit upon human consciousness.

Some kind of baptism (read: "initiation") is needed to
start the path to spiritual maturity. Fire, water, blood, failure, or holy desire may all be precipitating events, but

without a fall or a major dunking into the central mystery, a person has no chance of swimming in the right ocean. It is the necessary journey from the false self to the True Self. Without such a great defeat, we will misinterpret almost all religious words and rituals from our small ego position. We will use God instead of love God. Religion does not work at all unless there has been an encounter, especially a "close encounter of the first kind." We fall into an unnamable love, and a new freedom that many call God.

In the larger-than-life people I have met, I always find one common denominator: in some sense, they have all died before they died. At some point, they were led to the edge of their private resources, and that breakdown, which surely felt like dying, led them into a larger life. That's it! *They broke through in what felt like breaking down.* Instead of avoiding a personal death or raging at it, they went through a death, a death of their old self, their small life, and came out the other side knowing that death could no longer hurt them.

For many Western people, the life, death, and resurrection of Jesus of Nazareth is the preeminent example of this pattern, and he is often recognized, even by many non-Christians, as the most influential person of the last two thousand years. But the pattern is archetypal and hardwired in history, literature, and poetry. Jesus is a perfect exemplar of initiation in its full cycle. But there have been many others who have let "the single grain of wheat die" (a phrase found not just in John's Gospel but in the mystery religions of Asia Minor). Abraham, Buddha, Mary, Rumi, Joan of Arc, Gandhi, Martin Luther King, Mother Teresa, and the blood of all martyrs are the very fuel and

fire of history. In fact, if your life does not somehow exemplify this full cycle, you are merely helpful or interesting,
but not yet a *moshel meshalim,* a master of wisdom.

On some real level, all truly great people have faced
"the big one," and their greatness consists in knowing, as
my father, Francis of Assisi, did that any "second death
could do them no harm." This experiential knowledge of
death's lack of final power is the essence of every true initiation experience. Such people live in a different realm
beyond our usual fears, an alternative reality, different
than the one we take for granted. If you somehow make
that passover, then you are initiated. You cannot fake it
by any mere belief system, any moral performance, the
reassurance of belonging to a group, or any heroic endurance contest. Paul brilliantly lists all of these as the
usual counterfeits for love (1 Corinthians 13). I would say
they are the common substitutes the ego concocts when it
has not really passed over from death to real life. An uninitiated ego becomes rigid about words and rituals when
it lacks any real inner experience. There is a clear before
and after to an initiated person, and afterward you know
you are in a different psychic place; you are a different
person. (In some cultures, old debts and contracts did not
even apply to the newly initiated individual! You were
truly honored as a new creation.)

In most of history, the journey was taught in sacred
space and ritual form, which clarified, distilled, and short-
ened the process. It was not a lecture series. This is true
traditionalism, and it is the foundation of what we later
called sacraments. Life and its cycles initiate us similarly,
until we hopefully get the message for ourselves. Many do
not get it, I am afraid. They "rage against the dying of
the light" until the end. Since rites of passage and sacred

space have fallen out of favor in our consumer cultures, most people don't learn how to move past their fear of diminishment, even when it stares them down or gently invites them. They are not "prepared for the Passover" (Mark 14:16). I think that this lack of preparation for the passover, our lack of training in grief work and letting go, our failure to entrust ourselves to a bigger life, is the basis of our entire spiritual crisis. *All great spirituality is about letting go.* Instead we have made it be about taking in, attaining, performing, winning, and succeeding. Spirituality has become a show we perform for ourselves, which God does not need. True spirituality mirrors the paradox of life itself. It trains us in both detachment and attachment, detachment from the passing so we can attach to the substantial. But if you do not acquire good training in detachment, you may attach to all the wrong things, especially your own self-image and its desire for security. Self-interest becomes very well disguised, often passing for religion.

Primal cultures, those societies organized along tribal lines in Pre-Axial Consciousness, did not generally focus on the end of life or on last things. Fear of death, judgment, later reward, and punishment play very little part in their ways of thinking (unlike Christianity). Initiated and initiating cultures focused on getting the beginning right (thus the word initiation), and then they trusted that the end would take care of itself! *First things* instead of last things were their concern, and this focus makes all the difference in this world because it allows us to live in the present. It connects ordinary time to eternal time, uniting heaven and earth, rather than casting them as opposites, enemies, or one as a mere obstacle course for the other. I am afraid that moderns are utterly schizophrenic about the two worlds most of the time, except when we really love, really pray, or really stand naked in nature.

Our Christian word for this momentous first step is "incarnation" (the uniting of flesh and spirit), and it is the foundation for everything else, which then follows as logical consequence. As the early church fathers understood, "incarnation is already redemption," and you do not need any blood sacrifice to display God's commitment to humanity. Once God says yes to flesh, then flesh is no longer bad but the very "hiding and revealing" place of God. Then religion becomes much more an affirmation of life itself and love's possibility, rather than a funereal fear of death, judgment, and hell. True religion is always an occasion for joyful mysticism rather than a grim test of moral endurance.[13]

The social and structural genius of initiating cultures is that every generation was given a chance to start anew and afresh. It was the remaking of each generation of men, as a group and as a social unit. It was a salvation of history, not just of individuals. The work of regeneration cannot be done alone because we are essentially social, interconnected beings. Therefore regeneration cannot be taught by mere words or sermons. It needs ritual experience, community support, and even the minor mysticism of firsthand experience to get the fire kindled in each group. No wonder African American Christians emerge from the baptismal river singing "O Happy Day"! No wonder a man's life did not really begin until he was initiated. Until then he was unborn, a ghost, not a man. Afterward, he was not defined by any small and perhaps dysfunctional family or violent history. He was reconnected to the whole cosmos, realigned with the big picture (Christians, read "Kingdom of God"). He was now a son — and such cultures were not afraid to say it — a son of God! This is what Jesus knew at his initiation, his beloved sonship and the pleasure or favor of his Father (Matthew 3:17).

Regeneration's ability to bring us joy is radical and needed hope for our present world, which is largely defined by remembered grievances, tribal identities, and past history. With improved historical records and easy access to them, we actually have better reasons for hating one another, for anger and violence toward one another, than ever before! Terrorism is now defining the shape of history for generations to come — precisely because our generations experience no regeneration. The Indians dislike us more than they did fifty years ago, as do many African Americans and most foreigners. The cycle of violence seems to be the shape of our future. Without the spiritual regeneration of each generation, we are paralyzed by our past, and the future is only more of the same. The current religious tone is no more than a bad novel of crime and punishment.

Though both men and women are in need of initiation today, in this book I will be focusing on the initiation needed by the males of our species. Women more commonly had fertility or puberty rites because they matured in a markedly different way. Many cultures and religions saw the male, left to himself, as being a dangerous and even destructive element in society. For whatever reasons, the male did not naturally build up the common good, but invariably sought his own security and advancement as a matter of course. In some ways, women were historically initiated by their one-down position in patriarchal societies, by the humiliations of blood (menstruation, labor, and menopause), by the ego-decentralizing role of

child raising, and by their greater investment in relationships. Men have always seemed to need a whomp on the
side of the head, a fall from the proverbial tower, their
own blood humiliation (which became circumcision in an
amazing number of cultures), in order to become positive,
contributing, or wise members of the larger community.

As Ernest Becker argues so compellingly in his Pulitzer
Prize–winning book, *The Denial of Death*, the heroic projects of men are mostly overcompensations for a para-
lyzing fear of death, powerlessness, and diminishment.
Until men move into death and live the creative tension
of being both limited and limitless, he says, they never
find their truth or their power. As he shockingly put it,
we are overwhelmed that we are somehow godly and yet
"gods who shit."[14] Too often, egotism, performance, ambition, and bravado in the male proceed from a profound
fear of this failure, this humanity, this death, this shit.
The heroic project never works for long, and it always finally backfires into anger, depression, and various forms
of scapegoating and violence. In avoiding death, a man
ironically avoided life, and this central insight is what
animated the various rites of passage in primal cultures,
hoping to lead men into real life early in life.

Today young men try to self-initiate by pushing themselves to the edges and into risk in various ways. The
instinct for initiation is still there in young men, but usually not the wisdom nor the guidance to go the full cycle
and understand the message. We are finally healed by encountering "the real," which is precisely *everything* about
reality, warts and all. To forgive ourselves of everything is
the deepest kind of death for the ego. Such an initiation
into death, and therefore into life, rightly saved a man.
Catholics call it the paschal mystery or the passion of

Christ. The word itself is a giveaway, because passion *(pa-tior)* means to "allow" or "suffer reality." It is not a doing, but a being done unto. Today young men seek salvation through glib answers and heady beliefs in what Jesus did for them instead of walking the mystery themselves too. True religion is not about winning eternal life later by passing some giant SAT exam now. It is about touching upon life now, in this moment, and *knowing* something momentous yourself.

Classic initiation rites brilliantly succeeded in preparing men for both stages of their life: training young men for the necessary discipline and effort required in the ascent of the first half of life, and preparing them ahead of time for the necessary descent and letting go of the second half of life.[15] Today we do neither tasks of life very well, if at all, and institutional religion just keeps performing the first task of creating boundaries, identity, and ego structures over and over again. Ancient peoples saw that if men missed their initiation, they became unworkable human beings, for themselves and for the community. Every missed rite of passage leads to a new rigidification of the personality, a lessening ability to see, to adjust, to understand, to let go, to be human. It makes men finally incapable of the wisdom of the second half of life because they keep seeking the containment and private validation of the first half of life.

There is only one set of exceptions to this predictable narrowing and rigidification that takes place in people. Many handicapped and poor people, many people in minority positions, many who work with the dying and oppressed, most survivors of near death experiences, and true mystics in all religions are the glaring exceptions. They often grow more radiant, more flexible, and more compassionate with age. This is why the biblical tradition teaches that the "little ones" have a big head start in the ways of wisdom and spiritual initiation.[16]

If anyone tells you that you can be born again, enlightened, or saved, and going to heaven, and does not first speak to you very honestly about dying, do not believe that person. There is no renewal in all of nature without a preceding loss. Even the sun is dying every moment. You cannot be born "again" if you do not die first. The prosperity gospel is no Gospel at all. Death and life are in an eternal embrace, two sides of the same coin. We cannot have one without the other. It is the one absolutely common theme at the bottom of every single initiation rite that I have studied. Any initiation that does not experientially teach this paschal mystery is not an initiation at all.

Two

WHY WE NEED INITIATION
IN MODERN CULTURES

Lest we who have preached to others miss the
point ourselves.   — I CORINTHIANS 9:27

UNLESS A MAN has on some level been involved in the human struggle, it might be hard for him to know what is missing from society. You can only miss something that you have searched for and partially experienced. In fact you do not even search for it until you have already touched it. Now that classic initiation has been so long absent from Western society, we can do no more than point to the patterns of nature, the quick deconstruction of culture when it stops initiating, and some validating patterns in the very nature and growth of the brain.

We assume that animals imprint and pass on instinct more naturally than we do. But even our brothers in the animal world make it clear that juniors need elders to know who they are. Both humans and animals are imitative, or mimetic. We desire what others desire, and we do what we see others doing, even though it is humiliating for postmoderns to admit it. As Rogers and Hammerstein put it, we all "need to be taught, we need to be carefully taught." A few years ago there was a nature special on television about elephants in a certain part of Africa. For some reason, these young bull elephants were acting strangely out of character—antisocial and aimlessly vio-lent; they were stomping on VWs, pushing over trees for no reason, and even killing other small animals and baby elephants. Park rangers came in to study the problem and, in the course of their investigation, they discovered that there were no older bull elephants in that area. By some accident, all the older bulls had either died or been poached for their ivory, which left the teenage males to roam and forage out of control. Their solution?

They brought in some older bulls from other areas by helicopter, lowered them onto the scene, and in a mat-ter of weeks, amazingly, the whole situation had changed. Apparently, all the old bulls did was wave their ears and make various sounds or small charges, and somehow the younger male elephants understood through these com-munications that their behavior was not the way good elephant boys should act. It seemed to be just that simple. Things soon returned to normal once the elders operated as elders. In the human realm, when there are no "kings," young warriors become brutal, magicians behave as char-latans, and lovers are soon addicts. Someone has to give the young male boundaries and identity. He does not get them by himself or without guidance.

We are not a healthy culture for boys or men. Not the only reason, but surely one reason is that we are no longer a culture of elders who know how to pass on wisdom, iden-tity, and boundaries to the next generation. Most men are over-mothered and under-fathered — now even more in the age of single parents. Or to use the title of Alexander Mitscherlich's classic, we are a "society without fathers."[17] The effects of this are lifelong for both genders, creating boys who never grow up and want to marry mothers in-stead of wives, and girls who want securing and affirming daddies instead of risk-taking partners. Neither gender is ready for the work and adventure of a full life.

The current older generation of men in the United States has, to a great extent, not been mentored by their own fathers. They were usually given necessary messages either in quick male style or translated through the language and experience of women. Women have been training boys to be their version of men, or men who have not been mentored have been modeling a teenage level of ego development. Neither is what we need.

We are starting at zero now, in many cases, or praying for some act of spontaneous combustion, since you can pass on only what you yourself know. You can lead your sons and daughters only as far as you yourself have gone. Men who lost their fathers at age ten may do fine with their own sons up to the approximate age of ten, and then they often lose self-confidence in their parenting abilities. Following are just a very few of the sad statistics regarding young men who have not been mentored by elder men.

The patterns of failure among our young men are frightening; the levels of depression, suicide, drug abuse, alcoholism, and violence among young males today are exponential: "Over 94 percent of all inmates are male. Not only do men live an average of seven years less than women, but they suffer far more than their female counterparts from ulcers and other stress-related diseases. They are more likely than women to die sooner from each of the fifteen leading causes of death.... Over 80 percent of all suicides are men. In the twenty–twenty-four age bracket, males commit suicide almost six times as often as females. When men are over eighty-five, they are over fourteen times as likely to commit suicide as women of the same age. Men are hurting."[18]

For twenty years we were told that our whole education system was biased toward the success of boys and men, and yet now the results appear to be exactly the opposite. In recent years, girls have been surpassing boys in leadership positions, valedictorian addresses, graduation, and many of the more important jobs afterward. It is not politically correct to speak about this in many circles, the assumption being the opposite. Boys are succeeding largely at sports, but even there the young women are moving in, and boys' confidence continues to falter.[19]

You need a good bull elephant around or you won't know how to be an elephant at all. I was a jail chaplain for fourteen years in Albuquerque, and the only thing that almost all prisoners had in common was that *none* of them had good fathers.

Lest readers think that American society alone suffers from the lack of initiation for younger men, I must point out that even cultures as ancient as the aboriginal peoples of Australia have lost their traditions of initiation. Several years ago, I hosted a large men's retreat in Southwestern Australia. The men involved in planning this retreat had worked very hard to create a special time together, and part of their plan was to locate the retreat at a highly symbolic place near an ancient site, a place sacred to the aboriginal culture in that part of the continent for millennia. The name of the site was Kojunnup, which means "the place of the stone ax."

Nearby was a flint canyon, where young aboriginal men were led at the conclusion of their initiation rite. During this ritual, if they had shown themselves teachable and ready to handle power for the good of the community and not just for themselves, they were allowed to create a stone ax for themselves from the flint at that sacred spot. They returned ceremoniously to their village bearing their ax and their new mantle of manhood. In this way, their manhood was not self-constructed or privately possessed; rather, it was agreed upon and bestowed by the larger community of men and therefore was expected to be returned to the community in the form of service and participation. Mainly, it was a sign that the young man could handle power and not abuse it.

As good and inspiring as the process of initiation seems to have been for these young men of Kojunnup, the sad fact of history is that this five-thousand-year-old pattern of male initiation was undone in a very short time, and by one simple change. When the English and Irish settlers arrived, they gave axes to every young man—presumably so they could be more productive; one hopes it was not more malicious. But it undid the needed discipline and honor system. Soon young men who did not know how to handle power had power, and boys who had not paid any dues declared themselves men. The playing field had been falsely leveled. Young men who had no social vision or socially bestowed manhood were given power without being given the inner skills to know how to handle power. The result was that manhood lost its social dignity and spiritual influence, wreaking immense havoc on the whole ecosystem of that aboriginal culture, which lasts to this day. Is it not the same today when an already jaded sixteen-year-old is given the keys to a new car? Or when a young, fatherless black boy suddenly makes big money? Or when an immature American soldier is given absolute power over foreign prisoners?

The English historian G. M. Trevelyan said that Western education "has produced a vast population able to read but unable to distinguish what is worth reading." In other words, we have substituted job preparation for broad education, information for knowledge, facts and statistics for wisdom. What the primal peoples seem to have known is that mere technology without depth and breadth is dangerous, even destructive to society. Initiation was on a different plane than mere transference of facts and data.

One is hard pressed to find many great heads of government or even great statesmen in any of our Western democracies in recent decades—and democracy was supposed to allow the cream to rise to the surface. Nelson Mandela of South Africa and Václav Havel of the Czech Republic are some of the few, and neither of them was formed by a democracy. Too often those who rise to the top are men who have not been initiated into manhood through trial, community, or any public service and were simply given their stone axes of power and prestige because they had money, ambition, white skin, or a dad with a big stone ax of his own. This is not going to produce a great world. We must have purified cream rise to the top, not curds and whey. When the Vatican admits publicly that careerism and ambition is a problem among the bishops, as it did in 2001, we know that even the church, which is supposed to represent spiritual leadership, needs major reform. The church starts calling us "father" at age twenty-six, when all we have done up to that point is advance ourselves in status, security, and formal education, usually paid for by others. We have risked very little. Soon we are sincerely mouthing the rituals of death and resurrection at every Mass, while having had little or no practice in failure, poverty, diminishment, or surrender. It is a poor and heady way to form spiritual leadership.

The general assumption underlying all initiatory rites is that unless a young male is shown real power through a community of wise elders, *he will always seek false power and likely will spend much of his life seeking prestige, perks, and possessions.* This sounds exactly like Jesus's warnings and teaching when he sent his disciples on "journeys of vulnerability" (Matthew 10:5–42). The male power game parallels the story line of history, politics, business, and trade, and we cannot imagine it any other way. Is that why we call it *his*-story? Power, prestige, and possessions have been legitimized and idealized by every Christian culture I know of, all of Jesus's words to the contrary. How shocked I was when I first began to work with the Acoma Pueblo Indians in New Mexico in 1969, and I discovered a people who actually downplayed status, loved simplicity, and idealized the pueblo over the individual. And we thought we were bringing them the Gospel! No surprise that they still initiated their boys.

A bit of verification from brain science itself is in order. Recent studies of the human brain are yielding awesome results with major implications for child rearing, moral development, and information on why some people are ready for the big picture and some are not. We now know that what poets, lovers, and music lyrics always intuited is scientifically true; that is, that the heart knows much in neural, hormonal, and electromagnetic ways.

Joseph Chilton Pearce, in his enormously enlightening book entitled *The Biology of Transcendence: A Blueprint of the Human Spirit,* tells us that we have five brains all

together, and they build on one another.[20] At five approximate periods of human life (years 1, 4, 7, 11, and
14–17), we experience major brain surges where all past
experiences are stored and secured (in technical language, myelinated), and we become ready to connect
with the next higher brain. At each stage, we need models
of higher brain function in our lives to move ourselves to
that higher level of consciousness and conscience. Thus
good and mature people in our lives are important at
each of these stages. If you live around people at the "sex
and survival" level, or what I call the "lizard brain" level,
you have little chance of moving beyond the lizard brain
yourself, despite all the catechism classes in the world.
You might cooperate fully with your religious teachers,
but you will understand all the teachings on the level of
security, attractive self-image, and personal advantage—
while thinking you are a Christian, Jewish, or Moslem
holy man. It is not that we have not given people great
visions, but it is that *they use too little of themselves to see*
and, therefore, they do not see very far.

As teenagers we begin the last major brain surge, which
connects all four brains to the holistic heart brain, which
is probably why that first intoxicating teenage love is
so utterly romantic and forever idealized. Everything is
getting connected and myelinated, and we feel fantasti-
cally awake and alive! But if the right conditions are not
present at each stage, not only do we not connect with
the next brain level, but also we suffer one of the greatest tragedies in human biology: millions and millions of
unused cells die off, in a process that Pearce calls "neural pruning." It produces a kind of deep disappointment,
cynicism, and even rage in a young person. It produces
less conscious and less alert people. With the brain, it

is literally use it or lose it. Initiation and mentors protected society from this disaster. Wise elders around you actually reverse this strange law of gravity.

According to Pearce, a person's continuous, healthy development depends on being exposed during each period to people who provide nurturance and safe love, people who themselves live out of a higher brain and a bigger vision of life. *We need models of higher development around us to move forward.* We are socially contagious, especially in the teen years. This probably explains why initiations—confirmations and bar mitzvahs—were done in early teenage years in a community context. Once initiation rites stopped honoring this time-sensitive period, and once there were no real godfathers and godmothers, they became mere hocus pocus and empty ritual. In Catholic circles, there is often more concern about pleasing the bishop than transforming the kids. We are, it seems, both more biologically dependent and socially interdependent than the myth of the autonomous mind suggests.

In addition, brain development requires some degree of safe and loving human *touch*. Untouched infants and children simply stop moving through the brain levels and stop growing in other ways besides. Human beings have a kind of skin hunger. This surely indicates why any form of physical or sexual abuse at an early age is so devastating. The cells of the body know, remember, heal, and self-destruct according to the messages that they receive. For too long we limited consciousness to the head brain, but now we know that we are much more a *whole body brain*. Consciousness resides on many levels, and maybe that is why initiation rites were so holistic in their approach, not just verbal lectures. There are many ways of knowing yourself and your world.[21]

Such data about brain surges provides evidence for the excitement and enthusiasm that we see in most children. We are wired for transcendence and greatness, it seems. Watch it on the faces of high school students at pep rallies, sports events, and any group gathering. They are wanting and expecting and looking for greatness, significance, a compelling vision for life, a challenge, holiness, even God. Children and teenagers are unbelievably hopeful by nature; all of their life is out in front of them. If that big picture is not given to them — through contact with bigger people and at special windows of opportunity — young people will seek to fulfill the expectation in other ways: big crowds, loud music, marching armies, totally unrealistic fantasies, fame (or infamy!), money, and popularity. Anything loud, large, or socially admired becomes the substitute for the cosmic and the transcendent that they are really longing for. Someone needs to tell them that, even if they only half-believe it.

If there is no contact with greatness, there is an almost cosmic disappointment inside of us, a deep sadness, a capacity for cynical dismissal and sullen coldness, exactly as we see in so many of our young today. The visionary gleam is lost. It is as if they are saying, "There are no great people or great patterns. I will not believe in anything. I will not be disappointed again." It is called postmodernism, and it is the general assumption of our jaded and uninitiated society. But do note that it is not the presence of pain or suffering that destroys the brain; rather it is the lack of larger-than-life people around us. Primal cultures seemed to know that if young people missed being exposed to a greater meaning and greater people during key periods of their lives, especially the last clear opportunity at ages fourteen to seventeen, the result would be disastrous both for the young person and for the society.

Grace, of course, can finally prevail over anything, anywhere, anytime. However, today we have nothing in place structurally that will expose our young people to significance, and thus they miss the grace that is available in those critical years when they are most ripe for vision, breadth, and depth. I know for myself that it was my youthful dreams that set the runway for my entire life. They are still coming true, but in ways very different than I first imagined.

Ask yourself if that is not true for you too. Some young people may stumble upon this bigger vision providentially — reading the life of a saint or a hero, meeting a friend or mentor that invites them into the big picture. But I believe the lack of personal and social exposure to real depth and breadth makes most young people vulnerable to cheap religion, cults, and crowds as a substitute for largeness, hoping for salvation from their jobs or companies, selling their souls for fame and fundamentalism. All of which will die and eventually disappoint. All our youthful idealism, all our grand visions and hopes are practice runs and disguised desires for the great run for which we were created.

The momentum toward greatness is on the hard drive of our very brain. We were created for transcendence, and at our deepest level we all know it. But we have to install the software for one another. It is God's great gamble and our great responsibility.

Three

THE TWO BIRTHS

A neurotic could be defined as one who has failed altogether in crossing the critical threshold of his adult second birth.
— JOSEPH CAMPBELL

More than most people, I think alcoholics want to know who they are, what life is all about, whether they have a divine origin and an appointed destiny, and whether they live in a system of cosmic justice and love.
— BILL WILSON, FOUNDER OF
ALCOHOLICS ANONYMOUS

TWO PHRASES HAVE BEEN USED in the West to describe what we thought of as our spiritual initiation. Recent American Evangelicals use the language "born again," and historical Catholics used the phrase "washing away original sin." Both concepts are worth looking at to understand what was supposed to happen, and maybe why it often doesn't.

It seems that most of humanity intuited the need for two births: the first a physical one, and the second a spiritual one, which was necessary to make sense of the first. The phrase "born again" now tends to mean "a Southern USA version of the Christian message," or a person who has had a certain emotional experience. Someone who is born again usually has a moral and individualistic character, is tied to sets of words, and is extremely self-assured, often with a kind of warrior-for-God energy. Yet after the rebirth of authentic initiation, the effect tends to be much the opposite: *ecstatic, communal, earthy, and humble*—more lover-and-wise-man energy.

Jesus's term for such big-picture thinking was the "Kingdom of God" or "Reign of God," but we have altered it into "my" kingdom and my salvation experience. Being born again does not often feel like a rebirth but more like a continuation of the first biological and cultural birth, with some new buzz words added and some specific actions subtracted—drinking, cussing, gambling, homosexuality, abortion, and dancing being toward the top of the list, none of which Jesus talked about. Too often, there is little or no critique of one's false self, one's own country, or the closed culture of the born agains. This culture is not prepared to preach the Gospel to all nations because it frankly never leaves home, and it tries to bring everybody back there.

This rebirthing, three days in the belly of the beast or "night sea journeys," is classic mythological language. The Christian story that spawned the born-again language (John 3:1–21) is a classic initiation tale, where Nicodemus is the initiate who "came to Jesus by night." This makes sense since John's Gospel was likely written in Asia Minor where mystery initiations were the norm. The text says that to be born again is a pure gift from above, but also a laborious process on our part, like natural birth. Both are true. Initiation, as the word itself reveals, is the good and necessary start, after the Spirit both takes the initiative and completes the process. The Spirit never assumes you have already attained some objective state, the way born-again language does today.

True born-againness normally leads to *ego dispossession and immense charity for all.* It does not lead to tribalism and glib answers. Notice that Nicodemus only asks questions in the text. He gives no answers because he has none yet! He is searching for God, and he does not pretend to have God in his pocket. Our own personal holiness project must always diminish and our humility must profoundly increase in order for the Spirit to blow where it will.

It is worth noting that a hundred years ago the phrase "I am born again" was seldom used in the American South or around the world. This contemporary phrase is far too much of an ego possession and a group trophy. The more traditional language put the emphasis on God's status instead of our own. The older phrase was, "I was seized by the power of a great affection." I think the earlier version is much better, and it is similar to John Wesley's wonderful "my heart was strangely warmed."

ORIGINAL SIN

Borrowing from St. Augustine, the Catholic world used the somewhat confusing phrase "original sin" and the healing thereof to describe baptismal initiation. The very word "sin" bothers people here because we see newborns as innocent and pure, and we see sin as implying personal fault or guilt. The genius of the word's usage is that it actually reveals that sin is not always something we do as much as something that is done to us. It does not designate guilt for something we personally did wrong, but names and reveals what we all carry from the collective. It names the "corporate pain body" that we all suffer from together.[22] Original sin tells you not to be shocked or even surprised at the tragic flaw in all of us. People must not be naive about corporate evil, nor should they waste time blaming anybody, including themselves or their mother and father. Imputing blame is not the point; healing is, and you cannot heal something until you recognize that it is there. Mechanically understood, the doctrine is silly. Spiritually and psychologically understood, it is brilliant.

A large part of that collective pain body is passed on to us through our parents' wounds and hurts, just as it was passed on to them. As we say today, "It is in the genes." The church intuited the same when it taught that every parent, without exception, passes on some degree of original sin to their children.[23] The tradition said, rightly I think, that this wounding was healed by baptism. In other words, initiation into the large family revealed to the man that he was, in fact, a beloved son, even a son of God. He was ultimately validated from above. *The small family was no longer allowed to first or finally define you.* Letting go of the conditional parent-child relationship and accepting the unconditional parent-child bond is the heart of a true initiation, and it does indeed wash away the original wound, our endless capacity for self-rejection and self-hatred. True initiation is the passing on and personal claiming of a free gift and inheritance. The human collective memory and its store of remembered hurts must not be allowed to define us. In that sense, baptism and all initiation is sort of a preemptive strike at evil. "I" am bigger than my tragic flows, it says.

Without baptism into the mystery, we have no real future, only the fatalistic past—the original sin—to be lived over and over again. It takes the original blessing to undo and overcome the original sin, that is, the remembered and held collective pain. The intuition was perfectly correct, although healing this pain was seldom the result of the simple water ritual. But if your original wounding is not healed, every man you meet has to deal with the brokenness of your own father, and every women you meet faces your mother's unresolved issues—which you inherited—not to speak of your own store of personal memories and hurts. There also seems to be an ethnic heaviness that differs from culture to culture, probably depending on how well that culture has dealt with its own history of oppression and abuse. I believe that its degree of inner heaviness or inner freedom is a very good barometer of the health of a country's religion.

You don't need to call it original sin to know it exists. It is the tragic flaw of Greek tragedy and Shakespearean drama. It is the shadow self that you do not understand. It is the irrational, the nonsensical, the self-destructive, the suicidal, the inner split, the dark side that seems to be in everything. It was so real that most of history gave it full personification and just called it the devil. But certainly, original sin is our sharing in the common pain of being human. It does not need hatred. It needs healing. It does not deserve punishment. It deserves tears. It is not worked through as much as washed away by situating one's life in a much bigger picture. In that sense, I am very Catholic, although few Catholics understand it that way.

True baptism and initiation does indeed wash away original sin, and it does indeed give you a new birth and a victory over the power of death. True baptism allows us to reframe and contain the reality of evil, without blame or shame or vengeance. We are all in this together, and our common wound shows itself in different ways in different people. After authentic initiation, your surprise and false shock at human brokenness is stolen from you forever. You are beyond being scandalized and steeped into a scandalous compassion. It is no longer hard to live in a wounded world, in a sick body perhaps, and to bear the burden of our common and complicit humanity. I suspect that the body wound or scar that a boy always carried after initiation was his indelible reminder of this tragic flaw that is at the heart of everything.

Four

THE BIG PATTERNS
THAT ARE ALWAYS TRUE

Given the similarity of structure, sequence, and motive in the rites of passage among disparate and geographically separate cultures, one would have thought their ceremonies ordained by some central committee.
— JAMES HOLLIS

I NITIATION RITES may well be the oldest system of spiritual instruction known to us, and some form of initial rites of passage have been found in the overwhelming majority of primal cultures on all continents. Because holiness was first mediated through art, poetry, ritual, music, solitude, journey, movement, sexuality, fertility, and symbol, it is fair to say that initiation rites were the church and temple before church, temple, synagogue, and mosque ever existed. This is *the* tradition, and this needs to be preserved if you want to remain traditional or conservative.

The ideal goal of early cultures, conscious or unconscious, seems to have been to introduce young men to an alternative and ultimately more real world, so they would have a map and compass for connecting with this world. Initiation rites, therefore, contained most of the elements of mature male spirituality, and even a Judeo-Christian spirituality in its core elements of transformation. One of my major goals in this book is to make that clear, attractive, and compelling. Wouldn't such a pattern make perfect sense? "Grace builds on nature," as St. Thomas Aquinas said, and the Holy Spirit is clearly guiding all of history from the very beginning.

Sacred rituals and sacred words situated life in a bigger frame, so nature, beauty, suffering, work, sexuality, and ordinary humdrum were seen to have transcendent significance. Basically, they gave life meaning, and that is the one thing the soul cannot live without. Heaven and earth *have* to be put together or this world never becomes home. That integration is the necessary human and spiritual task, which initiation succeeded at, probably on a much broader scale than modern churches. So much so that many cultures had no word for religion. It was the same as life! This was the incarnation before the Incarnation! Jesus made incarnation particular, concrete, visible, and beautiful, but it has always been God's pattern and it is called creation. The word became flesh in space and time so we could fall in love with a concrete person and not just think about an idea. Yet the particular has always been scandalous and unworthy of thinking and sophisticated people.

Ancient Sanskrit and Hindu philosophy classically states the summary religious experience with three words: *Tat tvam asi.* I would loosely translate it as, "What is over there is the same as you." Jesus put it more personally: "I and the Father are one" (John 10:30) and more horizontally, "What you do to others, you do to me" (Matthew 25:40). One is not initiated until and unless one has overcome the dualistic mind—the great either-or. Union with God, union with *what is,* that is to say, union with everything, has always been the experiential goal of initiation. One taste, a free sample of the real, had to be given early in life to keep one hungry, harmonious, and holy. Otherwise, the whole human project is finally scattered and incoherent. It creates neurotics, rebels, and loners. Without a center point, the personality and the culture shoot out in all kinds of eccentric directions, particularly for the male of the species.

Initiation was always, in some form, a teaching about loss and renewal, darkness and light, the four seasons, death and resurrection, yin and yang, the paschal mystery. Only the words were different, and we are not here to say, "My words are better than your words." We are here to uncover what was deemed a universal and necessary experience. What superficially might look like exercises in determination, long-suffering, obedience, and moral heroics, in practice meant observing and surrendering your small self, your fears, your inadequate ideas, and your illusions about what matters. Somehow an initiate had to see the wide screen and, at least for a moment, find goodness and meaning in what was offered to him and right in front of him, which is all we can love anyway.

Although they might not have used the same word, there is a profound *contemplative* character to initiation. Universally, early cultures insisted on large doses of separation, silence, looking, and listening, and various kinds of suffering. Initiation was actually a temporary monastery for men, which cultures like those of Thailand, Japan, Tibet, and Burma have considered mandatory for the very survival of their societies.

The writer D. H. Lawrence seemed to understand these needs of the soul very well:

I am not a mechanism, an assembly of various
   sections.
And it is not because the mechanism is working
   wrongly, that I am ill.
I am ill because of wounds to the soul, to the deep
   emotional self,
And the wounds to the soul take a long, long time,
Only time can help,
And patience, and a certain difficult repentance,
Long, difficult repentance, realization of life's
   mistake,
And the freeing oneself from the endless repetition
   of the mistake
Which mankind at large has chosen to sanctify.[24]

Initiation rites might well be described as a brilliant form of that "certain difficult repentance" and the "realization of life's mistake." This is at the core of classic initiation—and psychological genius besides. Most scholars and historians of initiation seem to agree that the stages of initiation rituals are something like this. It has been called the "monomyth of the hero" because the pattern is so universal:[25]

1. Separation from business as usual, old roles, feminine affirmation, etc.

2. This moves the initiate, hopefully, into a "threshold space"

3. Here a numinous encounter is possible, desired, and required

4. Now the initiate returns to his community with a new identity and a gift for the community, although his primary gift is the man he has become

In my cross-cultural research on initiation rites, I have perceived five consistent lessons communicated to the initiate, and by and large they correspond to stages two and three above. These lessons are meant to separate initiates from their attachment to who they think they are, and reattach them to who they really are. The typical term for that new self is some kind of son of God or quite simply and finally *a man!* In fact, the boy was not a man until that point. A boy was initiated into manhood after he found his source, his validation, his reason for being, his foundation *in* being. We would say his place in the universe. Up to that point he was considered a boy, a nonbeing, a ghost, and a hungry ghost at that.

To be sure, not every rite contained all five of these lessons and, moreover, they were not expressed in my exact words. But the whole process tried to teach at least five truths about the nature of the universe and a man's belonging inside it. These are the five essential messages that a man has to know experientially if he is to be rightly aligned with reality. Remember, before we got it "into our heads," God and reality ("what is") were the same thing for almost all people who ever lived. The initiation correctly aligned the man, so he would not just survive in reality, but thrive. The process reflected the most foundational meaning of "salvation."

The entire process that we call initiation somehow made it possible for a man to experience these five essential truths. They became the five essential messages of initiation:

1. Life is hard.
2. You are not that important.
3. Your life is not about you.

4. You are not in control.

5. You are going to die.

You will perhaps be shocked by the seemingly negative character of these five truths, which probably shows
how untraditional we have become, even those who think
of themselves as conservatives. At this point in history,
we have some major surgery to do; separation from codependency, separation from limited self-image, separation from the autonomous ego, separation from the
securities of boyhood and an almost coercive push into
the responsibilities of manhood. This will appear negative and demanding to Western people. None of this is
easy work, especially when we have already become so
identified and addicted to these very illusions. Without
this hard training in detachment, we end up with what
we have today—fundamentalist silliness on the Right and
secular arrogance on the Left.

One wonders if history would have taken the violent
and oppressive forms it has if generations of men had
continued to learn these five lessons experientially. If a
critical mass or a cultural elite of humankind had experienced this enduring wisdom, this ultimate reality therapy,
it would have been a very different history. A dynamic
core is all we need to keep humanity from its gravitational
pull downward.

It is not surprising that a necessary critical mass was
invariably named as the key to spiritual survival. It was
variously called the remnant, the ten just men of Abraham, the apostles of Jesus, the leaven and salt, the church,
the enlightened community or *sangha* of Buddhism, the
umma of Moslems, Gurdjieff's conscious circle of humanity, the support group or Twelve-Step meeting of today.

Without a group, nothing goes very deep or lasts very long in the spiritual life. There is no outer corrective, confirmation, or natural teacher for the ego. When there is such a critical mass, the eccentric mind and individual willfulness cannot have the last word. Initiation tried to assure that the bottom line corrective of culture would be wisdom instead of money, success, and power. Today groups largely represent conformist unconscious thinking, and wisdom figures are relegated to the unheard edges. We can do much better, but the way up is first of all the way down.

Five

LIFE IS HARD

The Cherokee elder said to his son, "Why do you spend your time brooding, my boy? Don't you know you are being driven by Great Winds across the sky?"

You have to be sick and tired of being sick and tired before recovery can begin.
— TWELVE-STEP WISDOM

ALL GREAT SPIRITUALITY is about what we do with our pain. So the first lesson of initiation was to teach the young man not to run from pain, and, in fact, not to get rid of any pain until he had first learned its lessons. Human life could not risk being mere self-legitimation and pleasure-seeking; a man could not risk always taking the easier way or he would miss life's central and transformative pattern of descent and ascent, what Augustine called the paschal mystery. Creation has a pattern of wisdom, and we dare not shield ourselves from it or we literally will lose our soul. You can obey commandments, believe doctrines, and attend church services all your life and still daily abort your soul if you run from the necessary cycle of loss and renewal. Death and resurrection is lived out at every level of the cosmos, but only one species thinks it can avoid it—the human species.

In initiation ceremonies we see an almost universal emphasis on physical, emotional, and social trials. But most people stop there and never look for the actual message behind these trials. They think a daring raft ride down the Colorado or a stint in the army is in itself an initiation. It could be, but most likely it isn't. The real point is not an endurance contest, but a course in listening, waiting, and hoping, which has the effect of deepening and clarifying desire. This educates the emotional life, the inner world, the soul, which for some reason we don't think needs education as the mind does. Once you can grow in this way, you have an inner pattern for ongoing growth throughout your whole life. Everything will teach you and help you mature. As the prophet Jeremiah would say, the law will be intrinsic, "written within you" (31:33).

Initiation is not about being a warrior as much as it is about being conscious, awake, and alert. Note how much Jesus talks about the same issue, and "I am awake" is the very meaning of the name Buddha. Maybe that is why initiation was always done in nature and in various forms of solitude. Nature is the only thing that the young man *has* to respect. He cannot be larger than, above, or in control of nature. Nature's grandeur awakened him to mystery, and its silence silenced him. If a young man does not learn this respect early, he will spend his life demanding that everyone and everything listen to *him*, which creates a tragic deafness and narcissism. It inverts the nature of the universe. Alcoholics Anonymous is one of the few modern self-help movements that has the honesty to tell people that they are narcissists and selfish! Others dance around such an unflattering but obvious truth.

It is finally all about one thing: What are you going to do with your pain? Are you going to blame others for it?

Are you going to think that it has to be fixed? As the Buddha is supposed to have said, "Pain is part of the deal"! No one lives on this earth without it. It is the great teacher, although none of us want to admit it. *If we do not transform our pain, we will transmit it in some form.* Take that as an absolute. If we do not learn this all-important spiritual lesson, at least one, maybe all, of the following things will happen:

1. We will become inflexible, blaming, and petty as we grow older.
2. We will need other people to hate in order to expel our inner negativity.
3. We will play the victim in some form as a means of false power.
4. We will spend much of our life seeking security and status as a cover-up for lack of a substantial sense of self.
5. We will pass on our deadness to our family, children, and friends.

I am afraid that we have become very naïve about pain and suffering in America. "I don't have time for the pain," as the commercials say. Primal cultures were not so naïve, maybe because they had no choice. Advil and Excedrin cannot and dare not take all our pain away. One still sees the nobility of hardship in many poor countries and in ancient cultures like that of India. Most aboriginal peoples put us to shame with their simple happiness, patience, and endurance in the presence of difficulties. By trying to handle all suffering through willpower, denial, medication, or even therapy, we have forgotten something that should be obvious: we do not handle suffering; *suffering handles us*—in deep and mysterious ways that become the very matrix of life and especially new life. Only suffering and certain kinds of awe lead us into genuinely new experiences. All the rest is merely the confirmation of old experience.

It is amazing to me that the cross or crucifix became the central Christian logo, when its rather obvious message is aggressively disbelieved in most Christian countries, individuals, and churches. We are clearly into ascent, achievement, and accumulation. The cross became a mere totem, a piece of jewelry. We made the Jesus symbol into a mechanical and distant substitutionary atonement theory instead of a very personal and intense at-one-ment process, the very stages of love's unfolding.[26] Jesus became a cosmic problem solver, God became a petty autocrat unable to naturally love what he created, and Christian practice became a polite and fearful standoff instead of a cosmic love affair. We missed out on the positive and redemptive meaning of our own pain and suffering. It was something Jesus did for us (substitutionary), but not something that revealed and invited us into the same pattern. Once the transformational image of the cross was no longer working, we ended up with sick, complaining, and accusing Christian cultures, known much more for consumerism and addiction than the so-called pagan or tribal cultures.

It seems that nothing less than some kind of pain will force us to release our grip on our small explanations and our self-serving illusions. Resurrection will always take care of itself, whenever death is trusted. This is as certain as the sunrise. We dare not try to manufacture our own resurrections. It is the cross, the journey into the necessary night, that we must be convinced of, and then resurrection is offered as a gift. (Note that the tradition never says Jesus *rose* from the dead, but that he *was raised* from the dead!)

Parsifal's quest for the Holy Grail begins by entering the forest at "the darkest place." Dante beings his paradise journey "alone in a dark wood," and it continues through purgatory and hell. Darkness is the language of the mystics; it is what they call a "luminous darkness," which leads and teaches the soul. But for some reason, we all want light separated from any darkness. This central problem is revealed in the very first verses of the Bible, when God names every day of creation good, *except the first two*—the days when darkness is separated from light and when heaven is separated from earth are not called good (Genesis 1:3–8). Darkness and light dare not be separated! The real world, as Jesus teaches, is always a field of weeds and wheat, and we can never presume to eliminate the weeds (Matthew 13:24–30). It is a mere mind game, and a dangerous one at that.

Pain and suffering that are not transformed are usually projected onto others, eventually distorting or destroying personal relationships, the public mood, and even total institutions and eras. One can often feel "the pain body" in many individuals.[27] You can also feel it when you enter many rooms, groups, organizations, and even countries. As some say, you could cut it with a knife. It is almost a physical presence with physical characteristics. I can see why most cultures felt it necessary to personify the devil. We must recognize that unhealed wounds are not just suffered individually, but are suffered corporately and socially. Whether it is Germany of the 1930s, totalitarian Russian or Chinese communism, or the United States —

which seems to need a war around every ten years—untransformed pain takes over, and you become paralyzed against any higher life or vision.

Such people are very hard to convert. "Darkness covers the peoples," as Isaiah said (60:2). They cannot see or even desire the good, the true, or the beautiful because it is a threat to their comfortable darkness. I think this is exactly what Jesus means by "the sin against the Holy Spirit," the only sin that is impossible to forgive because no forgiveness is sought or deemed necessary. We prefer the familiar and the habitual because the new always demands the death of the familiar, which is where the ego hides so well. It is precisely this deliverance from evil that we pray for in every Our Father because it is a foundational blindness and hardness. The genius of initiation is that it offers not just individual and psychological healing, but structural and communitarian healing too—which is religion at its best.

Untransformed pain is usually sent out to lodge in some other place or person, as in the story from Luke's Gospel about the possessed man in the cemetery of the Gerasenes (Luke 8:26–39). All the nice people in town project the village's pain onto some plausible guy, and he is forced to carry the social burden and "live among the tombs." They have conveniently exported their anxiety to a place where they can easily hate it, just as we do in all our forms of racism, sexism, and imperialism. Jesus had to get this disguised and denied evil to show itself in visible and undeniable form—from his Jewish background, he rightly chose pigs! Then he sent *them* into the sea and returned the man to the village as a statement against them. How disappointing that the village's entire population asked Jesus to leave![28] The Gerasenes had found a way to live without their pain, and like most people, they created a credible scapegoat to avoid facing their own hard truths. Scapegoating actually works rather well — for a while at least — which is probably why we keep doing it.[29]

The cycle continues even today. America has become the scapegoat for the intolerable lives of the Taliban and Al Qaeda, and in turn, terrorism has become the all-purpose scapegoat for American fear and hatred. The precise issue or location of the scapegoat is largely arbitrary. A projection screen must and will be found, be it sinners, heretics, Jews, terrorists, communists, women, gays, blacks, or poor people. None of them are actually *the* problem or *your* problem; it is just that you need them to serve a purpose. Our negativity and fear must have a place to nest. The scapegoat mechanism quickly unites a group, as heads of state have always known, but since it is an avoidance of the real concerns, eventually our projected pain comes back to haunt us, and "the last state of the house is worse than the first."

In the spiritual life there is no elsewhere. First and last, you are your major problem. As the cartoon character Pogo said, "I have met the enemy, and he is us." My angers and irritations are, first of all, saying something about me, and that is what I must hear before I make any other judgments. But human beings will do everything under the sun to avoid the problems of *me, now,* and *here.* It is probably what we really mean by confessing our sins and embracing our shadow. It is very hard and utterly humiliating work. What rites of passage succeeded at very well was to hold young men's feet to this purifying and always unwelcome fire. They were circumcised and wounded themselves; they did not abuse or wound others, as the uninitiated always do.

What we have come to call sins are actually the *symptoms* of sin; in other words, they are the predictable effects of trying to live outside of evident reality, which is the cycle of death and rebirth. We prefer to feel appropriately guilty about the symptoms instead of doing the hard work of changing the underlying illusion, which is why most people don't grow very much. Guilt, in my opinion, is *never* from God. It gets us into a mechanical reward and punishment mentality instead of challenging us to ask, "What can I learn from this?" Guilt is often from the ego's need to think well of itself.

You can see why most Eastern and Native religions emphasized harmony, balance, and detachment as goals of initiation, instead of just providing a list of do's and don'ts, which don't necessarily send you on any kind of learning curve. A religion of do's and don'ts, in my experience, just leaves people in a continuous seesaw of deflation and inflation, with a strong undercurrent of denial and delusion. It is easy for us Westerners to see this legalism and violence in Islam, but a little harder when it takes a Jewish or Christian form.

The search for balance and harmony was the more primitive way of keeping us safely inside the always-truthful paschal mystery of Jesus, even if they called it yin and yang, darkness and light, winter and spring, angels and demons. It takes a contemplative mind to be content with paradox and mystery. The daily calculating mind works in a binary way; either-or thinking gives one a sense of control. The small mind works by comparison and judgment; the great mind works by synthesizing and suffering with alternative truths. The ego cannot stand this suffering, and that is exactly why it is so hard for religions and individuals to grow up. *The ego prefers a satisfying untruth to an unsatisfying truth* because the ego demands instant satisfaction and the settling of all dust.

Initiation was not moralistic at all. It was mystical and contemplative. It unveiled the Great Spirit in all things, and then we were able to live with all the seeming contradictions.

TRUE SELF/FALSE SELF

Anyone who wants to preserve his life must lose it, and anyone who loses it will actually keep it safe. —LUKE 17:33

The very important question, therefore, is which self can we lose and which self needs to be preserved. For too long we thought it was the physical self that had to be lost, and the soul, or spirit, would, for some unknown reason, automatically emerge. Don't believe it. Show me where that is true. Let's try instead a framework of true self and false self.[30] Our false self is who we *think* we are. It is our mental self-image and social agreement, which most people spend their whole lives living up to— or down to. It is all a fictional creation. It will die when we die. It is endlessly fragile, needy, and insecure, and it is what we are largely dealing with in the secular West. The false self is inherently fragile and needy because it has no metaphysical substance whatsoever. It is formed entirely in psychological and mental time and changes or dies easily. *Yet most people spend their entire lives projecting, protecting, and maintaining this fiction.* The false self is passing, whimsical, and utterly preoccupied with self-maintenance and not much more. It is not your life at all, but merely your life circumstance passing for you. Once you learn to live as your true self, you can never be satisfied with this charade again; it then feels so silly and superficial. Yet we are still tied to our false self by years of training and habit.

The false self must be destabilized or we will never know the true joy of being, which is inherent and natural. What all religion is saying, in one way or another, is that human beings seem to be living with a tragic case of mistaken identity. A natural deconstruction of the false self tends to begin in midlife, although sometimes earlier if one has experienced limit situations. If we live and die right, we gradually will fall back into who we always were, but had forgotten during the climb and arrogance of youth. This often leads to peace in old age. Initiation merely tries to direct, facilitate, and speed up the process of rediscovering our true self. Its work is reconnecting, realigning, and regrafting us to our true identity because "the branch cut off from the vine is useless...cut off from me you can do nothing" (John 15:5). The false self is a privately manufactured and maintained "I am." The true self is our participation in the great "I Am." It is what Peter daringly calls "the ability to share the divine nature" (2 Peter 1:4). The true self is indestructible and characterized by an inner abundance. It is not needy, easily offended, or hurt. The true self is characterized by contentment, an abiding low-level peace and happiness, although now and then it becomes pure joy. It knows that *all* is okay — despite it all. You can't earn your true self because you have it already—which is why many people resort to exultant Alleluia language when the discovery is finally made. Hear the Jesuit poet Gerard Manley Hopkins describe the joy of the unveiling of his true self:

> These things, these things were here,
> And but the beholder wanting;
> Which two when they once meet,
> The heart rears wings bold and bolder,
> And hurls for him,
> O half hurls earth for him off under his feet.[31]

If religion does not introduce you to who you already are "hidden in God" (Colossians 3:3), then religion is a part of the problem and not a part of the solution. In that case it keeps you trapped in both your illusion and your guilt, while foolishly calling that good news, which it clearly isn't. It keeps you codependent on the fixtures of religion instead of encouraging you to joyously draw from the abundant fountain of God. Healthy spirituality leads you back to the garden, which is the archetypal image of lovemaking, intimacy, and fertility, but always through another garden—Gethsemane.

Religion is about one thing—making one out of two. It does nothing else. "Make your home in me as I have made mine in you," Jesus says (John 15:4). Religion is about Adam returning home, going back to where he started. You might even say that the entire Bible is about getting Adam back to his beginning, back to the garden that he foolishly left. All of this parallels the classic and universal journey of Odysseus, Parsifal, Dante, Buddha, and John Bunyan.[32] The pattern is always the same. But it seems we must go through a thousand circuitous and tortured routes before we "return to where we started and know it for the first time," to use T. S. Eliot's delicious phrase.

THE SACRED WOUNDING

Grace creates the void that grace alone can fill.
— SIMONE WEIL

When life is hard, we are primed to learn something absolutely central. I call it God's hiding place. The place of the wound is the place of the greatest gift. Our wounds have a chance to become sacred wounds. As C. G. Jung succinctly put it: "Where we stumble and fall is where we find pure gold." No surprise that a dramatically wounded man became the central transformative symbol of Christianity. Once the killing of God becomes the redemption of the world, then forevermore the very worst things have the power to become the very best thing. Henceforth, nothing can be a total dead end, and everything is capable of new shape and meaning. Henceforth, we are indeed saved by gazing upon the wounded one — *and loving there our own woundedness and everybody else's too* (John 3:14, 12:32, 19:37). It becomes a world that is grounded in mutual vulnerability instead of any need to impress one another or even to impress ourselves. It is the core meaning of the Christian doctrine of Trinity — the very inner shape of God is mutual deference and recognition and not self-assertion.

The heart is normally opened through a necessary hole in the soul, which is what the wound symbolizes. "One of the soldiers pierced his side with a lance, and out flowed blood and water" (John 19:34). It is the only way, it seems, for us to get out of ourselves and for grace to get in. As Leonard Cohen put it in his most important song, "Anthem," "There is a crack in everything, and that's how the light gets in." If there were another way, "I would have told you so," Jesus put it (John 14:2). Our wounds are the only things humbling enough to break our attachment to our false self and strong enough to make us yearn for our true self.

I could not find a single example where a young man was not symbolically and actually wounded and scarred in initiation rites. It was most often circumcision, but there were other forms of ritual humiliation too. It gives a depth of meaning as to why Christianity worships a pathetically wounded man — which is a most unlikely, disappointing, and even unsatisfying image for God. It must be answering a central human problem and the core of the human dilemma, maybe more than we consciously know. Spiritually, everything seems to hinge on one finally crucial question: "What will a man do with his wounds?" But have no doubt, *a man must and will be wounded.* When we no longer know that, we look in all the wrong places for salvation, and we end up with what we largely have today—a winner's script religion—in which nobody really wins. Our wounds do not become sacred wounds because we do not admit having them.

NAMING AND MARKING

"Your name shall no longer be called Jacob, but Israel, because you have wrestled with God and won!"…The sun rose as he left, limping because of his hip.   — GENESIS 32:29, 31

The discovery of one's participation in a true self is often expressed through the symbol of taking a new name, and so it is probably no accident that *naming* continued to be associated with both circumcision for Jews (Luke 2:21) and with baptism for Christians. The religious instinct, as usual, is correct, although the primitive meaning is invariably lost. Initiation moved one from an old self to a new self, entailing a new identity and a new operative persona. We see this change from Abram to Abraham, Sarai to Sarah, Jacob to Israel, Saul to Paul, and Simon to Peter. In each case it was a change of destiny, reference point, and vocation, always because of some inner breakthrough experience.

All studies of initiation that I have read are very clear about a before and an after of initiation. In fact, if there is not a strong sense of difference, one has not been initiated! We Catholics also had a practice of taking a new name at the time of Confirmation, often the adoption of the name of a personally chosen patron saint. (I took Philip when I was confirmed at age ten because I wanted to be joyous like St. Philip Neri was supposed to be.) This is likely a leftover of the new identity and new name that initiation was supposed to symbolize.

A group of us were deeply moved at a recent Rites of Passage that our team gave in Leicestershire, England. At the end of the wonderful event, the stiff-upper-lip English men stood bare chested and declared a proud "I am" before their full given name in front of the whole group. Then we anointed their heads and chests with handfuls of sacred oil and blessed them as beloved sons. Many of the men were overcome with deep emotion at the very dramatic pronouncing of their full name publicly. One could feel a deep recovery of dignity and identity as usually happens at the end of initiation, yet it was the same name they had always had — but perhaps really didn't know. A man's name, like his penis, somehow represents his essence in a distilled and sacred form, and we are always searching for its deeper and broader truth.

In some places, the authentic symbolism of naming and initiation persists. On a recent trip to Kerala, South

India, I came upon several newborns in Christian families. When I asked for their names, the parents would firmly say, "No name!" and I was confused. The child is apparently observed for several days and weeks after birth, and has no social or significant identity until both observed traits and God's call come together and are noted by a formal naming at the time of Baptism. But not before.

The same is true in the Native American vision quest, where the initiate cannot return to the village until he knows his sacred name and has met the Great Spirit. Perhaps this pattern of self-discovery of one's true name in God is the heart of the matter of initiation. (See Revelation 3:17.) The same instinct is found between lovers who often give themselves or one another their own secret pet or bedroom name. It is intimate, personal, sexually charged, and would perhaps sound silly — except to the two lovers. Friends share nicknames in much the same way. I have spiritually directed people who have a secret and sacred name that they use for God or a name that they hear God call them — a pretty clear sign that one has indeed passed through primal religious encounter. Where such a personal name exists, there is usually an intimate I-thou relationship at work. "I am not my own. I am intrinsically named as a beloved by the gaze of the other." It seems we cannot fully name ourselves. We are named through a relationship with another, like the Trinity.

We are not just named; we are also usually marked on our body, like Jacob being wounded on his hip by the angel. The wound always says that we have gone the distance and completed the necessary cycle: "I can take it, and I am not a victim." Remember, Jacob continued wrestling until he got a blessing, yet the main blessing he got was the ability to wrestle all night while he had an injury to his hip! This is very telling spiritual literature. Somehow the message has to be written on our very body so we will never forget it, and our body itself becomes a lifelong sermon, reminding us that our wound is our blessing. Handicapped people have this potential head start over the rest of us, and many of them take advantage of it. I wonder if the present need for hazing, tattoos, and body piercings is not the secular substitute for what young men once sought by fasting, circumcision, scarification, shaving of heads, and knocking out of teeth.

Unfortunately, these rituals have largely become social ceremonies where a chosen name is given and the ritual is performed, but there is no strong sense of a change of identity or the discovery of one's inner and sacred name that comes with true transformation. As John the Baptist said of himself, we tend to baptize with water much more than with "the Holy Spirit and fire" (Luke 3:16). Maybe we are still following the religion of John the Baptist more than the religion of Jesus.

The change from the false self to the true self is so significant and metaphysical in its revelation that Catholics even spoke of some of the sacraments as having an indelible mark. The new name, the water rite, the ancient slap, the full body anointment with chrism, the sign of the cross — all were external markings on the body, just as circumcision might have been before, to remind us of an internal change and of our dignity being carried in our actual physical self. True initiation marks you indelibly and gives you your sacred name, but only when it is accompanied by a sacred wounding that reminds you forever that life is hard.

Six

YOU ARE NOT IMPORTANT

How can a gnat dare to be reverent?
— COVENTRY PATMORE

O God, if I worship you in fear of hell, burn me in hell. If I worship you in hope of paradise, shut me out from paradise. But if I worship you for your own sake, do not withhold from me your everlasting beauty.
— RABI'A, ISLAMIC MYSTIC AND POET

DURING A RECENT preaching tour in India, I was taught about the difference between a school, a retreat house, a house of prayer, and an ashram. Although all the others can be held together by assigned roles, salaries, boards of directors, and vision and philosophy statements, an ashram entirely depends on the presence of a master, an enlightened person, whom the others would call a guru. In fact, if there is not a local guru, a true ashram does not exist or will not last. I visited several deserted ashrams that were patiently waiting for the emergence of a wise and holy person to animate the place again.

Unfortunately the word "guru" has been cheapened by media usage in America, but it is a very sincere and sacred term for Indian people. Quite simply, a guru is a master in the ways of holiness and transformation into holiness. But the key is that he is both medium and message; his life is his message. Much as when Jesus says, "I am the way, the truth, and the life," or when Paul says, "Imitate me." This is not egocentricity; it moves the whole process to the personal, relational, and lifestyle level (some would say energy level), out of the head and the theoretical. It is also why some holy people heal you merely by touching you. Their message is their transformed person, unlike a book or some ideas. Maybe it is why Jesus never wrote at all. He must not have been too concerned about mere verbal orthodoxy; in fact, he says as much (Matthew 7:21, 21:28–32). Right words make all of us feel falsely important; right action keeps all of us forever beginners and not so important at all.

Lifestyle and relatedness is more important than words, or as Francis of Assisi is supposed to have said, "Preach the Gospel at all times, and when necessary use words." We may reach out through media and technology or through our written or spoken message, but we finally transform and initiate each other through *who we are.* Transformed people tend to transform people. In fact, we tend to be able to lead people only as far as we ourselves have gone.

It is relationships that change us much more than ideas. We cannot really do something until we have seen someone else do it; it cannot yet enter our mind as a possibility. You do not know what patience is until you have met one truly patient person. You do not know what love is until you have observed how a loving person loves. What power we have for one another! For good and for ill. Thus rites of passage were communal rites, led by elders and father figures, and not sermons or a series of questions and answers — very low-risk encounters and forms of education, which the churches have relied upon for centuries.

THE WAY A MASTER TEACHES

The way a master teaches is different than the way an educator does. Not only does a master teach by his very person but by moving quickly and directly to the essence of a lesson, as opposed to the mere passing on of information or technique. A master has the authority to put the punch line of enlightenment right at the beginning, not at the end, moving immediately to the core, the heart of the matter, avoiding all explanations, nuances, softening, or clearing away of difficulties for the unwilling ego. Plop, an instantaneous truth lands right there in the middle of your pond, like Basho's frog in his classic haiku:

> Breaking the silence
> of an ancient pond,
> A frog jumped into the water—
> a deep resonance.[33]

Spiritual masters are not interested in social niceties or logical buildups, but in deep resonance. Consider Jesus's very first lines in Mark: "Time's up! The Kingdom of God is right here. Get a new mind. Believe some good news!" (Mark 1:15). Masters say, as it were, "Deal with it. Be scandalized and shocked. Face your resistances and your egocentricity right up front and let a greater truth unsettle you." They lead their students into a space of transformation, but they don't always lead them back. They leave you alone, deliberately askew, without your usual mental protections — until you long for guidance and hopefully recognize that: (1) you are somehow the issue, (2) the answer is within you, but (3) you need help from a higher power.

Don't waste your time theorizing, projecting, denying, suffering paralysis, or avoiding your own ego resistance. The master is not afraid to give you a dose of humiliation to determine whether you are even at a kindergarten level yet. If you immediately balk at a minor ego humiliation, the master knows that no basic transformation into your God Self has taken place yet. It takes a master to teach you that you are not that important; otherwise, painful life situations have to dismantle you brick by brick, decade by decade. Since we no longer accept or trust spiritual teachers, we are stuck almost entirely with the second and slower form of learning. I suspect that the basic reason that initiation died out is because there were not enough masters around. We had to settle for institutionalized priests and ministers, roles of authority instead of people of authority.

An honest reading of the Gospels reveals that Jesus taught in this same way, and as a layman! But we have stopped hearing a lot of things from him. Our defenses are up when sacred Scriptures are read. (It is like when you stop listening to your mother because you think you have heard it all before and because she does still have power over you.) Jesus knew that he needed to destabilize a person's false self before they could understand that they had a true self, but destabilizing our security systems and our ego is always a hard sell. "What does it profit a man if he gains the whole world and loses his soul," he says (Luke 9:25). He sets up a difficult either-or choice, "You cannot serve both God and mammon" (Matthew 6:24). This is vintage master teaching.

Typically, it is the prophets who deconstruct the ego and the group, while priests and pastors are supposed to reconstruct them into divine union. As Yahweh said in the inaugural vision to Jeremiah, "Your job is to take apart and demolish, and then start over building and planting anew" (Jeremiah 1:10). True masters, like Jeremiah and Jesus, are both prophets and pastors, which is why their teaching is almost too much for us. They both deconstruct and reconstruct. But the only reason they can tell you that you are not that important is because they also announce to you your infinite and unearned importance. Maybe the reason we cannot speak the first truth is that we no longer believe the second. We can no longer properly humiliate our small self because we no longer believe in the great self. Our personality and self-image is all we have. That is the problem of a secular culture. We end up crawling over one another and competing with one another to defiantly assert our private importance, which is our only possession.

Every master's lesson, every parable or spiritual riddle, every confounding question is intended to bring up the limitations of our own wisdom, our own power, our tiny self. Compare that, if you will, to the Western educational approach of parroting answers, passing tests, and getting grades, which make us think *we do know* what is important and, therefore, we are important. Information is seen as power, as opposed to the beginner's mind, which wisdom deems absolutely necessary for enlightenment. Jesus called it "receiving the kingdom like a little child." To submit to being taught means accepting the greatness of truth and our own smallness in relationship to it, instead of holding on to the illusion that we have or can master truth by getting an A! A master drives you toward the substance so you will stop defending and protecting the forms. A master acknowledges what you do know, but never lets you forget what you do *not* know.

We have strong ego structures in defense of our momentary form if we have not yet touched upon our substance. Why wouldn't we? A master is so committed to substance that he or she feels free to ignore, subvert, expose, or even humiliate our physical form. Most Westerners will no longer tolerate this defeat, because form and style tend to be all we have. Just observe any magazine rack at any airport and see how image, style, personality cult, and passing dramas feel like the only game in town. We appear to be lost in a whirlwind of images, all passing and changing week by week. Amazing that people bother with it and let it clutter up their minds and hearts.

When I go to the hermitage, I try to separate myself from all newspapers and magazines for a while, and it is amazing how little I have missed when I return. A master reminds us that we must not get lost in these passing spectacles and dramas; they are exactly what we are not. The Buddhists call it the principle of impermanence: All forms are passing away. "What vanity it all is, and mere chasing of the wind" (Ecclesiastes 2:11), the Hebrew Scriptures say. All is a passing diversion and distraction, especially if it keeps us from the one true thing. Admittedly, a certain amount of diversion is probably necessary for survival. One cannot live moment by moment with the full body blow of painful or even wonderful reality.

In America we would ask the masters what right they have to talk to us in their way, or how they can presume to know us so well and give such hard advice. If I tried to talk to most people the way several wise people have talked to me, they would say I was not listening to them or that I was arrogant. A holy man in India warned me before he prayed with me, "Are you prepared for the translator to hear your sins?" I gulped. I was not sure that *I* wanted to hear my sins! Who cared about the Hindi translator? This Catholic holy man, although young, was a master teacher and seer, and he told me in the next hour and a half things he could not have known through any normal channels. It is what St. Paul called "the gift of knowledge" (1 Corinthians 13:8). He moved right to my essence, gave me very direct and even hard advice, then moved me quickly and closely to the heart of God. By giving me a vivid sense of how I was being used largely in spite of myself, revealing my lack of faith and gratitude, he also invited me into something larger and greater than myself with a supreme naturalness. He did not try to humiliate me, although he did reveal some of my sins; he was not moralistic at all, and 95 percent of the message was almost embarrassing in its affirmation and validation, mostly by clarifying God's greatness in my life!

I was affirmed by being reminded that I was being used. I was criticized for taking it for granted. My value was something that I *participated in,* and nothing I could claim or defend as my own. I walked away knowing God was good, and by implication I knew that I was good too — though almost by accident. It was a *shared and reflected goodness,* which made me fall in love with God anew and take myself less seriously than before. This is the masterful way in which a master teaches. In his presence, I knew I was not important at all, yet more important than I had ever imagined. That's the paradox!

PAYING NO DUES TO LIFE

You boldly settle all the important questions. But tell me, my
dear boy, isn't it because you are young and the questions of
the world have not hurt you yet?
                              — ANTON CHEKHOV, *THE CHERRY ORCHARD*

A gathering of American teachers told me recently that in
their high school classes, students are not at all interested
in writing papers or doing research on objective information. Rather, they just want to give their feelings and
opinions on data and information. They love to say what
they like and do not like about things — as if everybody
should care! And this is students aged sixteen and eigh-
teen. We are inflating the youthful ego in ways that will
not serve them well during the rest of their lives — in relationships, in marriage, in future job performance, and
surely not in the search for God. Western and comfortable people everywhere have a strong sense of deserved
entitlement, and we are creating unsolvable troubles for
young people by enabling such a sense of entitlement,
usually in the form of cheap but effusive affirmation. "I
am special" buttons and "We are number one" banners
pinned on young people who have done little or nothing for themselves or society only trivialize the human
project. It dumbs the whole thing down to an embarrassing and finally unworthy image of their real dignity and
possibility. From people of whom so little is expected, little
can and will be expected for the rest of their lives.

A master intentionally leaves a student in the belly
of the whale, on the horns of our dilemmas, struggling
with parables, with problems, riddles, and koans (a form
of Zen riddle that is ostensibly a contradiction, but only
in the old mind). The ego must be frustrated until the

student's self-serving and learned logic begins to crumble and he or she begins to call upon the deeper resources of a larger mind and heart. The two recognitions often happen at the same time: When I am not king, then the kingdom has its best chance of breaking through. When I am king, it is a closed system. We must help people to get out of their own way, and we can't do that without help! Powerlessness is the beginning of wisdom, as the Twelve-Steppers say.

All we can finally do is pray that we allow the flow of desire, which is the very presence of the Spirit within us. If there is no living water flowing through you, then you must pray for the desire to desire! As a priest, my constant disappointment is the lack of spiritual desire and even spiritual curiosity in most people. I meet a lot of fearful people in church, a lot of opinionated people, a lot of "don't bother me" people, a lot of people seeking roles and importance through church ministry, but I honestly meet very few who truly seek God. In my experience we largely gather those who seek security in religion (which is not to say that they are not good people). Initiation rites attempted to pull back the veil from reality to expose a larger world of wisdom and mystery—thus stirring an unquenchable desire—and a high-risk journey to satisfy that desire. Once the desire for something more is stirred and recognized, it is just a matter of time. Nothing less will ever totally satisfy you again.

Seven

YOUR LIFE IS NOT ABOUT YOU

The important religious question is not that of the rich and young man, "What must I do to inherit eternal life?"

The essential religious question is the one God, in effect, asks Adam, "Who are you? and Whose are you?" We like the first question because we think there is something we can do about it, and it gives us control. We fear the second question because only God can answer it, and his answer seems too good to be true.

THE THIRD ESSENTIAL MESSAGE of initiation is usually learned after the fact and almost subliminally, even though it is a seismic shift in consciousness. You know, after any true initiating experience, that you are a part of a much bigger whole. Life is not about you, but you are about life. You are not your own. You are an instance of a universal and even eternal pattern. Life is living itself in you. You have been substituting the part for the whole! It is an earthquake in the brain, a hurricane in the heart.

Accepting that your life is not about you is a Copernican revolution of the mind, and it is just as hard for the individual today as it was for earthbound humans when they discovered that our planet was not the center of the universe. It was unimaginable, and the church condemned poor Galileo as a heretic for imagining it. To know that your life is not about you is a major and monumental shift in consciousness, and it is always given and received with major difficulty. It comes as an epiphany, as a clap of the master's hand, as pure grace and deliverance, and never as logic or necessary conclusion.

Understanding that your life is not about you is the connection point with everything else. It lowers the mountains and fills in the valley that we have created, as we gradually recognize that the myriad forms of life in the universe are merely parts of the one life that most of us call God. After such a discovery, I am grateful to be a part — and only a part! I do not have to figure it all out, straighten it all out, or even do it perfectly by myself. I do not have to be God. It is an enormous weight off your back. All you have to do is *participate!* "How could a gnat dare to be reverent?" After this epiphany, things like praise, gratitude, and compassion come naturally — like breath. True spirituality is not *taught;* it is *caught,* once our sails have been unfurled to the spirit. Henceforth our very motivation and momentum for the journey toward holiness and wholeness is immense gratitude for already having it! (Think about that, please.)

Initiation, as we have been speaking of it, is an entirely different genre than almost all other forms of education and catechesis that we have today. The only settings that would be similar are ongoing spiritual direction, the Ignatian/Jesuit Spiritual Exercises done correctly, the Tibetan monks' debates (where the goal is not to win but to keep smiling!), the desert monks planting cabbages upside down, a long pilgrimage without plan or money, or perhaps time in jail or under persecution. In each of these cases the small self must be exchanged for the big self to succeed or survive, and then, ironically, success itself is utterly redefined, and survival is no longer considered very important at all.

I am convinced that the reason we Christians have misunderstood many of Jesus's teachings is that we have not seen Jesus's way of education as that of a spiritual master. He is trying to situate us in a larger life, which he calls his Father, pure and simple. But instead we made him into a scholastic philosopher if we were Roman Catholic, into a moralist if we were mainline Protestants, or into a successful and imperialistic American if we were Evangelical. Yet the initiatory thrust of his words is hidden in plain sight. Study, for example, the instructions for the twelve as they are commissioned by Jesus to go forward and spread good news. Note that it was not an intellectual message as much as it was what we used to call an "urban plunge," a high-risk Outward Bound experience where something new and good could happen. It was designed to change the men much more than it was meant to change others! (Matthew 10:1–33, Luke 10:1–24, or "Mark's Catechism" from 8:31–10:45). Today we call it a reverse mission, where we are ourselves changed and helped by those who we go to change and help.

What is all this Jesus talk about going barefoot, taking nothing for your journey, having only one shirt, staying at whatever house accepts you, eating what is set before you? Is this really a sustainable pattern for one's whole life? Did Jesus actually intend Christians to live this way? I would argue not, although my first Franciscan brothers surely tried, as did the Mennonites, Amish, and many other individuals along the way.

When read in light of classic initiation patterns, Jesus's intentions are very clear. His message was not meant to be a pattern for one's whole life, but it was to serve as a school, a training ground, a boot camp in basic insecurity and trust. He was trying to present the values of a life of vulnerability in which one would have practical and needed experience of the same. It would be a life without baggage so one would learn how to accept others and their culture instead of always carrying along our own country's assumptions and calling them "the good news." He did not teach us to hang up a shingle and try to get people to attend our services, but exactly the opposite, that we should stay in their homes and eat their food! This is very strong anti-institutional language. One can only imagine how different history would have been had Christians done this boot camp training. We might have borne a message of cosmic sympathy instead of cultural and military imperialism, dressing ourselves down instead of dressing up for our worship services, providing humble reconciliation instead of religious wars and the murdering of heretics, Jews, and native peoples in the name of Jesus. We learn slowly, but fortunately God seems very patient. Maybe God has gone through his own boot camp, since God hardly ever gets his own way. God must be very familiar with letting go, since God's creatures insist on being in control and important.

When we could not make clear dogma, moral code, or a practical war economy out of Jesus's teaching, we simply abandoned it in any meaningful sense. His training of novices has had little or no effect on church style or membership, by and large. When one throws out initiatory training, the whole latter program and plan of life is left without foundation or containment. We seek a prize of later salvation—instead of the freedom of present simplicity. For this reason, the Sermon on the Mount —

the essence of Jesus's teaching — is the least quoted in
official Church documents in history, though there were
always people like Francis of Assisi, Simone Weil, Menno
Simons, George Fox, Catherine of Genoa, Peter Maurin,
and Dorothy Day who made it their life map.

They all knew that lifestyle was more important than
theories, intellectual belief systems, or abstruse theology.
Once you know that your life is not about you, then you
can also trust, as Gandhi did, that "one's life is one's message." It gives you an amazing confidence — and what
might even look like brashness — about your own small
life — precisely because *it is no longer a small life, it is no
longer just yours, and it is not all in your head.* Henceforth
you do not try to think yourself into a new way of living,
but you first live in a new way, from a new vantage point —
and your thinking changes by itself.

One story from his life has Francis of Assisi climbing
to the roof and tearing off the tiles of a humble house
that the friars had built for themselves. This was certainly
not a very nice thing to do to all those sincere followers
of his. I wonder what the dinner conversation was afterward? Did his band of followers understand that this
deconstruction of a building — and of themselves — was indeed their initiation at the hands of a spiritual master?
Did they understand that his brashness was not pride or
arrogance, but an apparition of a larger life? Could they
let go of their little ego hurts and defenses at that moment? If so, it would have been most rare. If they did hear
him, it was because they knew his life was not about him
and theirs was not about them.

I sat right next to Dorothy Day once in the early 1970s
when we were both speakers at the same education conference. She was not dressed especially well, made no

attempt at social niceties, dove right into her peculiar vision for education, with her seeming naivete, assaulting the system, and still got a sincere and deserved standing ovation. I followed her at the podium, trying to please everybody with lovely ideas, and got a more than polite applause. Dorothy taught like a master; I taught like a teacher. She had the authority of her life and her lifestyle, which allowed her to critique without being negative or judgmental. I might have said more astute things than she did, but she changed lives that day. I doubt that I did. As Pope Paul VI loved to say, our world will no longer believe teachers unless they are first and also witnesses of what they teach. Mother Teresa could just say "God loves you," and the whole crowd would believe it! We knew that her life was not about her. Her energy converted us much more than her words.

In summary, true initiators, saints, and agents of transformation exemplify a total cosmology, which has the effect of making psychoanalyzing, rationalizing, and moralizing unimportant; it is no longer necessary, and sometimes not even interesting. One is introduced to the One Life, and my smaller life is now a matter of lesser importance. I am less concerned about how, when, where, and whether. A new, larger self takes over. It is all about getting your true self right. "Who are you?" is the master's insistent question.

Who I am, and the power that comes with the response, answers all my questions. Life becomes a joyful participation in Being. We ride as willing partners in Paul's "triumphal procession" (2 Corinthians 2:14) instead of indulging in self-preoccupied attempts to get it right or in gazing at one's always disappointing navel, or even in new explanations of why I am the way I am. All the gazing is now at the goodness, all the riding is now on the

coattails of life and death, all the explanations are un-
necessary. Because it all goes on with or without me, so
I might as well go along.

My life is not about me. It is about God. It is about a
willing participation in a larger mystery. The great Paul
of Tarsus said it well, as he did so often: "The only thing
that finally counts is not what human beings want or try
to do, but the mercy of God" (Romans 9:16). Whatever
you think of St. Paul, and I am sure you are beginning to
notice that he is one of my heroes, he was without doubt a
fully initiated man. His urgent and passionate journey, his
love that was both self-effacing and utterly self-assured,
made it clear that his life was no longer about him. You
don't have to agree with all of his conclusions to know
the magnanimity of his soul: "I live no longer not I," he
shouted with his one daring life (Galatians 2:19). And
this one-man show turned a Jewish sect into a worldwide
religion. He allowed his small life to be used by the great
life, and that is finally all that matters. Your life is not
about you. It is about God and about allowing your life to
"be done unto you," which is Mary's prayer at the beginning and Jesus's prayer at the end. Which probably makes
it the only prayer worth saying:

> This is what the saints know and we don't.
> This is why we don't really understand the saints.
> This is why masters cannot teach many people.
> This is why there are not many masters.
> Most people think their lives are about them.
> And they aren't.

Eight

YOU ARE NOT IN CONTROL

At some moment I did answer Yes to Some-
one — or Something — and from that hour I
was certain that existence is meaningful and
that, therefore, my life in self-surrender had
a goal. — DAG HAMMARSKJÖLD (1905–1961),
U.N. SECRETARY GENERAL

A PHRASE THAT DOMINATES much of the self-help jargon of our society is "take control of your life." To be in control of one's destiny, job, or finances is an unquestionable moral value today. It even sounds mature and spiritual. On a practical level it is true, but not on the big level. Our bodies, our souls, and especially our failures, teach us this as we get older. We are clearly not in control. It is amazing that we have to assert the obvious. This is not a negative discovery but, in fact, the exact opposite. It is a thrilling discovery of one's fate, divine providence, being led, being used, one's life having an inner purpose, being guided, having a sense of personal vocation, and owning one's destiny as a gift from God.

Learning that you are not in control situates you correctly in the universe. You cannot understand the joy and release unless you have been there. You come to know that you are not steering this ship. It is essential if one is to feel at home in this world, and it is found in all classic heroes, mystics of all religions, and Christian saints. They

67

know they are being guided, and their reliance upon that guidance is precisely what allows their journey to happen. What perfect symbiosis! (See Romans 8:28ff. if you need confirmation.) The tragic hero, in classic theater, is precisely the one who ignores or denies this destiny or this guidance, because of hubris or pride.

But I must warn you; it will initially feel like a loss of power, a humiliation, a stepping backward, a silly dependency. The Twelve-Step programs have come to the same counterintuitive insight. You must get through that most difficult first step of admitting that you are powerless before you can find your true power. What a paradox spirituality is, and what a humiliation for the imperial ego. It is the necessary and universal starting point for a serious spiritual walk, which probably tells you that true spirituality will never fill stadiums and seldom creates cheering crowds. If it does, it is surely not the Gospel or any true wisdom tradition.

The spiritual teacher must loosen the novice's grip on his own projects, his exclusive self-directedness, and his willfulness. This loosening was done through training in being led and taught, through various forms of schooling in obedience, and through working with an elder. This was the only way to destabilize the ego's natural self-will, which wants total control. We see this willfulness in very little children. As Gerald May, one of my own teachers, so rightly says, willfulness must become willingness in the world of the Spirit: "Willingness implies a surrendering of one's self-separateness, an entering-into, an immerson in the deepest processes of life itself. It is a realization that one already is a part of some ultimate cosmic process and it is a commitment to participation in that process. In contrast, willfulness is a setting of oneself apart from the fundamental essence of life in an attempt to master, direct, control, or otherwise manipulate existence."[34]

I have often said that the virtues in the first half of life are quite rightly about self-control, and in the second half they are about giving up control. More dramatically, in the first half of the spiritual journey we fight the devil, and in the second half we fight God. That has become evident to me as I have grown older. It seems to have been evident to the poet Rilke, too, although he said it much better:

> How small are the things we choose to fight.
> What fights *us* is so great!
> If only we could let ourselves be overcome,
> As nature is overcome by a great storm.
> Because if we do win, it is a small victory,
> And the victory itself makes us small.
> Whoever is defeated by an angel,
> Always goes away proud and upright, full of strength,
> And greater still for having felt his power.
> This is how we grow:
> By being decisively defeated by ever greater forces.[35]

Remembering that initiation rites attempted to give a young man the essential life messages early, even before he was fully ready to hear them, we can see such rites universally tried to prepare a young man for what I call the great defeat, the necessary recognition that you are not really running the show, and *any attempt to run it will ruin it.* The intense self-will of the autonomous ego must eventually be disillusioned with itself. Having total control, and even the value of being in control, is a major desire and illusion in the early years of life, yet many hold on to it until their last breath. Try practicing to release control early; it will make your second half of life much happier. Practice in small ways, and gradually you will be ready for greater efforts, until you are finally ready for the big letting-go called death.

In the same way, classic initiation tried to prepare a young man in small doses for the recognition that he did not need to be in control. They did it negatively, forcing him into the inevitability of the laws of nature, and positively, giving him a sense of destiny and vocation. He had to feel chosen, guided, and used, which of course is exactly how the entire Judeo-Christian tradition got its initial momentum—through people like Abraham, Moses, Joseph, Isaac, Jacob, and Paul. None of them were perfect men. Most of them were downright immoral in one or another way, but they allowed themselves to be *used* (read "chosen") despite the humiliating evidence against them. I think that is the likely meaning of Jesus's enigmatic line, "The many are called, but very few are chosen" (Matthew 22:14).

As St. Therese of Lisieux so brilliantly put it, "If you are willing to *serenely bear the trial of being displeasing to yourself,* then you will be for Jesus a pleasant place of shelter." Thank God, they made this twenty-four-year-old, uneducated French girl a doctor of the Church. She is a master teacher who was never afraid of humiliating evidence about herself, which she called her "little way." What gives religion such a bad name is that most religious people are eager to be pleasing to themselves, and they like to be a part of a big way. It is my daily battle.

This depth charge of wisdom — powerlessness — was often taught by subjecting the young seeker to periods of extended silence and solitude, usually accompanied by fasting—experiments in surrender, understimulation, and nonperformance — so one could plug into another source. This normally had to be done in nature, so the young man could participate in "the only thing greater than yourself," as Kunte Kinte's father said when he raised his newborn son to the skies. No surprise that acts of nature are called acts of God; they are the one thing we do not try to sue over. Nature is one place we will, for some reason, surrender our control, and not get too angry.

The young man was also trained in very practical ways — shocking to us — by various forms of trial, communal life, and hierarchy. If learning that your life is not about you meant reeducating the intellect, learning that you are not in control meant reeducating the will. Somehow he had to practice not always getting his own way. He had to learn very young that often much better things could happen when he did not try to predict and control all outcomes. *Predictability might be good for science, but it is not helpful for the soul.* The lesson was too crucial to wait for one's marriage and children, one's failing health, or one's deathbed to teach it to us. Much of Western history since the Enlightenment has been committed to throwing out most notions of obedience, training by elders, communal life, or hierarchy. They were beneath our dignity. The totally self-determined life became the only life worth living, nearly the opposite of the entire history of spirituality. One wonders where our assurance about such things has come from.

OUR FLAT EARTH SOCIETY

The leveling down of humanity into a herd, by suppressing the natural aristocratic or hierarchic structure, will inevitably lead sooner or later to catastrophe. For if all that is distinguished is leveled down, then all orientation is lost.   — C. G. JUNG

While in India I was amused at the common practice of marriages arranged by parents and grandparents, even in educated and sophisticated families. When I tried to defend my case for our style of dating and romance, the couples rose quickly to their parents' defense. As one young mother put it, "It all depends on whether you want the previous generations to set the tone or you put that decision in the hands of those who are just starting." In a flash, I got it.

India, like much of the East, has not bought so easily our Western notion that freedom and equality, as we understand them, will solve all social problems. Instead they look in the direction of respect, humility, and mutual honoring, an Eastern wisdom we can clearly perceive in Jesus's teaching. In fact, I don't think Jesus ever talks about equality — except for knowing, teaching, and assuming that all people are absolutely equal children of God, recipients of the same inheritance, and universally enjoying the common divine indwelling. This is the firm and life-giving foundation for everything else he teaches and for the full meaning of all political justice. It makes you indestructible personally because your dignity is inherent and not earned. Theologically we are absolutely equal, and only healthy religion is prepared to make that claim, which is why I cannot give up on religion. But political equality is secondary, and paradoxically, as we saw with communism, any idealized notion of political equality can actually lead you to destroy this first divine equality and dignity in others, and therefore in yourself too.

Americans have made equality into a marvelous piece of political theory, but I do not believe that anybody really believes in it on a practical level. There is clearly a hierarchy of the wise, a hierarchy of the powerful, a hierarchy of the healthy, a hierarchy of the virtuous, a hierarchy of age, a hierarchy of the attractive. If not, we would have no capacity to judge anything, no point in growing or developing or learning, because there would be nothing to develop toward. Indeed, if everyone were equal in this sense, just about everything exciting in the world would collapse into a boring blandness. No more Olympics, no more great literature, no more fine art, no solid philosophy, no more idealizing of quality anything, no critique of this book; the songs of the Beach Boys would be deemed as good as Beethoven's symphonies, Rodney Dangerfield's worldview would be seen as valuable as Thomas Aquinas's; there would be no moral difference between the oppressed and the oppressors, no scales, criteria, reference points, or measures. There would only be a postmodern flat earth society, a moveable famine. Can we not see this tendency toward blandness in today's popular culture of malls, chain stores, derivative art, general dumbing down, infantile television, and hate talk radio?

Even though God gives us different starting points, it is *our* obligation to give all people equal opportunity to develop and grow, whatever their starting point. The whole universe is nothing but differentiation, with each part having both its special powers and its areas of total vulnerability. Birds cannot write or calculate math, but they can fly. Humans can think and do math, but they can't live exposed on earth, in the air, or in the water. Only the humble duck can walk, swim, and fly, and so the Native peoples said that ducks are actually God's favorite? Who knows where the power really lies and who is God's favorite? All we know is that we are all a part of some wonderful whole, and we are all wonderful in different ways.

It seems the entire universe is participatory, and yet also hierarchical, according to both quantum physics and integral philosophy. They do not seem to contradict one another. Ken Wilber makes a brilliant distinction between "actualization hierarchies" and "domination hierarchies."[36] Actualization hierarchies are parents in relationship to children, bodies in relationship to cells, hosts in relationship to parasites. The smaller needs the larger for its very existence. Nothing in the universe survives without such a protective hierarchy, according to Wilber, and in fact, it is the only way to protect growth and create wholes. We hate the hierarchy of government taxes, yet we love the hierarchy of government security systems. We can't have it both ways. "Without actualization hierarchies you have heaps not wholes, strands but never a web.... *Hierarchy and wholeness, in other words, are two words for the same thing*," he says![37] Jesus would call it servant leadership, I think.

Domination hierarchies, however, do not really support or sustain those on the lower levels. The leaders merely control them by various forms of coercion, guilt, or social pressure, and make them codependent on them (which many people confuse with help!). We are so mistrustful of and angry at domination hierarchies, after centuries of the abuse of power, that we deem the very word "hierarchy" a bad word, even though we desperately need actualization hierarchies to survive and thrive. Our postmodern and postfeminist world fears domination, and I understand why, yet it acts as if there is nothing good about elders, obedience, tradition, leaders, or authorities. This is not serving us well, and it is part of the reason for the overreaction of the neoconservatives in both politics and religion. I would, of course, think Jesus was again on the mark. He never rejected or abdicated leadership; he simply grounded it in servanthood and community rather than in domination (John 13:12–15, Luke 22:24–27). What genius. Jesus is never out of date and always up to date.

Uniformity is based on some level of coercion, but true unity is created from diversity by love, which is why the Spirit creates true unity. If the mystery of the Trinity is the first template of all reality, then what we have in a trinitarian God is the perfect balance between union and differentiation, autonomy and mutuality, identity and community. Isn't that almost always the problem? Think about it. True love differentiates and individuates; it does not create slavish conformity. When you are loved rightly, you are more yourself, your true self, than ever. In true unity, "The eye does not say to the hand 'I do not need you'" (1 Corinthians 12:21). However, that does not mean that the eye must become just like the hand. Coercion works only in the very short run; it is love that works in the long run. God seems to trust the freedom that leads to real love and is willing to wait for a very long time to achieve that kind of love.

The Gospel, therefore, is not a flatland, but "many gifts making *a unity* in the work of service" (Ephesians 4:12), each deferring to one another out of mutual recognition, like the Shakers dancing and bowing before one another. If we deny that some people are natural leaders, some have an inner authority, some have experience and education that we need, we are in serious trouble. Elders must take their proper role and youngsters must recognize that they need it. In our topsy-turvy world, we now have elders envying and imitating the young! When actors, wrestlers, people who have no history of public service,

money makers, and cowboys are the personalities who
are elected heads of state, one wonders what the advantage of a breadth and depth of experience and education
might be. One wonders if democracy will finally work in
an uninitiated culture that admires the values of youth
and not the values of maturity. My sense is that the older
generation has not spiritually grown up themselves—they
were not initiated either and are therefore not elders but
merely elderly.

As a Franciscan, dedicated to a simplicity-loving and
egalitarian worldview, I never thought I would promote
the importance of hierarchies and nobility, but the alternative that I have seen is a disaster ("dis-astra" = discon-
nected to the orientation of the stars). If the bottoming out
that we have in popular culture today were the lovely biblical idealization of the *anawim* (the poor and humble) it
would be wonderful; however, I am afraid what we have
instead is a glorification of the crass, the cliché, the clever,
and the superficial, instead of the simple and humble. It
is not the holy, the well educated, or people with a nobility of purpose who set the tone; rather we are inspired
by that which makes money. This is getting us nowhere.
Robert Bly rightly calls it a "sibling society."[38] It tends to
dumb down instead of evolve up.

Previous history surely had its major blind spots, but in
being up front about class and caste, nobility, hierarchy,
and even royalty, it was at least possible to confront and
even abolish such status positions when they were abused
or no longer doing their job. Quality people finally create
quality control by setting higher standards. Initiation believed that nobility could be taught and greatness could
be passed on. Traditional cultures thought that educated

and big-picture people had to be allowed to be the ones to set the tone. Class was not just about making money, as it largely is today, but about personal depth and breadth, skill, training, exposure to life, faith, and even manners. Quality control was structured into society through initiation, and elders took their proper role as bearers of a heritage of wisdom. Does it not seem that the present generation of parents and older people have abdicated this role? They substitute recent cultural and religious small traditions for the great tradition. Could it be because they do not know much about history or the larger world themselves? That is what drives me to write this book. My aim is to present the great tradition here, which most people are not familiar with.

DO THE ELDERLY HAVE ANYTHING TO SAY TO THE YOUNG?

I was a part of that flippant generation that said, "Don't trust anybody over thirty." Now I have turned sixty, and it all looks very different. But why did we say that in 1968? Were we just arrogant or did we sense something that was partially true and very disappointing to us? We were longing, I believe, for wise mentors, but our elders did not appear enthusiastic about anything that really mattered. For all of its superficiality and secularism, I do believe our generation in the 1960s was, unwittingly perhaps, trying to rediscover some very traditional Judeo-Christian values that had been socially ignored up to then: human and civil rights, nonviolence, political and gender equality, love for other races, other religions, and others in general, along with a capacity for self-criticism. In our own immature way, we 1960s folk were trying to self-initiate because our parents' generation, in our view, had substantially sold out to materialism and militarism.

The real religion of America has always been America itself; our religion has largely been civil religion for the sake of social order more than for any soul transformation. Our parents, raised in that heady, rising tide of the first half of the twentieth century, had little to teach us in terms of origin, foundation, and goals. They gave us what they had been given in place of a true initiation, the self-serving American dream of material advancement and an overreliance on religious institutions to do our spiritual work for us. Instead of a transformational journey, we were offered two nice systems to belong to: *pro Deo et Patria,* religion and country.

How could we not confuse America with the kingdom of God? On our dollar bill, the eternal eye of God is just about to rest on the almost completed pyramid of our empire. Below it is written that we are the *novus ordo seclorum,* "the new order of the world," and *annuit coeptis,* "[God] favors what we have begun." Such an identification of the United States with God's kingdom, and the pride and arrogance that go with it, remain part of our national consciousness, even if most Americans can't read Latin. Just ask any Canadian or Mexican, our closest neighbors, and increasingly more and more of the world.

In response to this profoundly unsatisfying civil religion, plus our lack of initiation where no one shaved our heads and took us into the woods, we instead let our hair grow long and went into the urban jungles in the 1960s. Too much structure always calls forth some anti-structure. It is as predictable as the sunrise. No one taught us wisdom, so we listened to Simon and Garfunkel, read

Beat poets, and searched out maharishis from the East. I remember hanging around the radio in the seminary listening to the words of "The Sound of Silence," and my classmate saying, "The words actually mean something!" All we had heard for the previous ten years was "Shooby dooby doo."

Without question, we were resorting to peer initiation, and predictably the results were mostly shallow and short lived. The '60s generation did not go deep with their insights, nor lay any philosophical or theological foundations for them. Cynicism soon set in, and we are now often as materialistic and militaristic as our parents were. Yet some of the critical thinking of the '60s became enshrined in a maturing conscience and human rights awareness that we now take for granted—even those who call themselves conservatives. God even uses Balaam's ass to get the needed message through, as you remember (Numbers 22:22ff.). It is the Spirit guiding history, and that Spirit will not be thwarted. All we can do is refuse to offer our cooperation or seek to turn back to the "good old days." As if God were back there but not here.

Many young people and clergy today long to return to an earlier and false innocence that never really existed. I understand their psychological need. We must start with some experience of order, or we will not have the ego structures to move forward. In the first half of life, the psyche demands structure before it can possibly deal with antistructure.[39] They want to return to a romanticized church and world of the past that they idealize from a distance. They hope that it will provide the clarity, status, and certitude that they do not enjoy and that their ego needs. It is no surprise that so many young men resort to the military as the only remaining bastion of true

Americana. While the liberals have rejected authority in favor of a specious equality, neoconservatives, longing for some kind of stabilizing order, are on bended knee before presidents, popes, and principles. I had that desire myself when I was young, growing up in 1950s Kansas! That is the only reason I can talk this way now. We all need some still point in the midst of the tornado of postmodernism. But the trouble is, all the biblical God ever promised us was God himself as that still point, and never any institution, role, constitution, social order, army, leader, or country. These are human-created idols that we worship in the place of God.

In the absence of any still point or any real eldership today, seventeen-year-olds turn to other seventeen-year-olds for pseudo initiations, and young turks in the business world seek help from other young turks in the same business world. The blind leading the blind, I think. The late Ronald Johnson, who worked with black boys at risk in California, quite rightly says, "The whole country is filled with gangs, and not just street gangs, but AT&T gangs, Enron gangs, Pentagon gangs, Capital gangs, Bishop gangs."[40] In a sibling society that is ungrounded and uninitiated, deprived of depth or height, one can only live on the horizontal and codependent level. When one does not believe in something, we will fall for anything — and with bravado. The psyche needs and demands some central reference point, and we will create one to calm our neurotic and restless imagination. If God is not the one, then the Dow Jones Index and Rush Limbaugh will be. We *will* have a "one."

In other words, if a man has not been authored from above, he will give his authority to the crowd, as Pilate did. He will allow a foolish and cruel young woman to justify murder, as Herod did with Salome. He will sell his soul for a sardine, as Teresa of Avila put it. It is not surprising that we created the word "codependency" to describe the postmodern self. We are willingly influenced by spin doctors; in fact, we fully cooperate with them. Without an experience of the absolute, we are all "reeds shaking in the wind," as Jesus said.

WHERE DO WE BEGIN
IF WE ARE NOT IN CONTROL?

Neither an immature denial of all authority nor a slavish adherence to law and order will work for us anymore. We must find true authority both within and then also without. But where do we go to be "authored"? For starters, we must recognize, honor, and make use of the wise people who are already among us. There are plenty of such sages around us, but they may not be highly visible or in positions of influence. Transformed people do not necessarily seek external roles or power because they have power at a deeper level and use it automatically by just being who they are. They are inherently *life-giving,* and they are what Janet Hagberg describes as people with "real power."[41] Power goes out from them, as the Gospels say of Jesus.

People who have let life initiate them tend to be creative individuals, grounded and solid. You can feel it when you are in their presence. You feel safe and you feel energized. They do not take your energy; they give you energy. You know they have an excess of life, and maybe some for you, so you seek them out, as the crowds did with Jesus and still do with wise men and women. A wise man does not need to wear a uniform, badge, title, or special hat to tell you that he has authority. Her spiritual authority is obvious as soon as you talk to her, which is not to say he is a perfect person. So don't look for that, or you will always be disappointed. Being chosen and being useable are not the same as sanctity — that is absolutely clear in the Bible. It just makes it easier for *us* when they do coincide. In fact, I usually find that most great people still carry one or another significant personality flaw. It is fairly predictable. St. Paul himself, clearly flawed, humbly recognized his "thorn in the flesh, an angel of Satan to buffet me" (2 Corinthians 12:7), which he says was necessary to keep him "from getting too proud." In most wise people I know, their very authority and wisdom come from the struggle itself. A neurotic genius is to be expected.

The greater light you have, the greater shadow you often cast, C. G. Jung said. Maybe this is why Peter is consistently presented as a flawed and ordinary human being, while still proclaimed by Jesus to be a rock.[42] *Ordinary men and women can and should serve as our mentors.* They need to be spotted, sought out, and supported as such. We need to set up our own "Tuesdays with Morrie," as times to be taught, and not wait for experts or official classes. The search for the perfect is usually the enemy of the truly good. You can take that as an axiom for all of life.

In spending these last fifteen years of men's work trying to spot and support older men, I have done my small part to initiate many men, and then I sit back and wait to see who does anything with what they have been given. Is this just another personal growth experience, another notch on their belt of spiritual credits, or does this man go out from the experience to care about his neighborhood, his church, his sons, nephews, and godsons? Does he really recognize that he is a part of the cycle of generations? Does he remember what we taught him, that his life is not about him? It soon becomes clear who the natural elders are — *after* initiation.[43] Many men are, of course, still elders in the making, or as we say in men's work, princes and not kings. So we keep working with the princes. It takes quite a while to become a king, and is generally not reached before your mid-fifties.

MALE LOVE NEEDS TO BE EARNED

The mature person loves with both the motherly and the fatherly conscience, in spite of the fact that they seem to contradict one another....In the failure of this development lies the basic cause for neurosis.   — ERICH FROMM, *THE ART OF LOVING*

Because initiators did not give away privilege, status, and respect cheaply, youth were made to earn them. The same thing happens in the military, sports, and early-stage patriarchal religion. There is an ego-structuring nature to male love. It is tough love, but still love in a way that a male respects and honors—as long as it is not cruel or demeaning. In later years, men largely recall and remember their tough teachers and their demanding coaches, those who pushed them to their best and their limits. In some way, a male knows that his other teachers did not take him seriously—and he did not take them seriously either. They needed his love more than he needed theirs, and he knew it. Such love loses its power for male redemption. Many women, soft men, and present humanistic culture do not understand this. *Males need to need and work for male love.* Love does not work for the male when it is given away too cheaply, too quickly, or too easily. It turns him into a lazy manipulator instead of a strong man.

We see this same tension in the New Testament, where the Gospel of John has Jesus rather frequently saying things like, "*If you keep my commandments, you will remain in my love*" (John 15:10). His love seems very conditional. I am convinced it is a necessary balance — although a seeming contradiction — to the many stories and passages that show Jesus always taking the initiative in loving sinners, outcasts, and the unworthy. Which is the true Jesus? I think both are true, and both *need* to be true for love to be love.

At its best, father love is also conditional. Such love serves the child well outside the picket fence, where he must eventually go to school, a job, and a partnership in marriage. The unique quality of such love is that it gives the boy impulse control, ego boundaries, and a sense of his own identity and power: "I can do something to acquire it: I can work for it; I can improve myself. Father love is not outside my control as mother love usually is."[44] This is not a bad place to work from, and it has many life benefits, as long as you have unconditional love somewhere. Perfect unconditional love is found only in God, of course. It is more than enough to heal all your woundedness if you know how to access it.

The healthiest people I know had a combination of both conditional and unconditional love from their two parents. It is an unhelpful myth that constant unconditional love from both parents produces strong ego structures, healthy people, or necessary impulse control. The most effective organizations, I am also told, have both a "good boss" and a "bad boss." We need the sacred "no," something to butt up against, something to create limit situations for us, or we never go deep and demand the best of ourselves. Parents must love us enough to allow us to be angry with them and fight them now and then. Organizations must have laws and someone who enforces them, or we all slip back into private self-interest. God clearly loves us with both left and right hands, total demand (commandments) combined with pure, unearned grace. It helps us grow up, and we are held securely inside reality.

Personal discipline and internalized values were never assumed in the young man historically. In fact, they were assumed *not* to be there until they were taught, demanded, practiced, and tested. In this sense, the military is much smarter than most progressive schools or liberal anything. The privileges of manhood are given only to those who have paid some dues to the common good, and therefore can be trusted not to abuse the common good. Otherwise, we merely empower selfishness. Historically, very clear distinctions were maintained between levels of advancement and status in the community. The elders, who had earned certain privileges, did not need to justify them to the young, whereas the young needed something to work toward and achieve. This serves the growing boy very well. It *is* a meritocracy, which the young man inherently respects, even though he fights it all the way. This is precisely the meaning of the law in the Bible, although most people make it the final goal.

The male, for some reason, does not respect anything that he gets for nothing. I spent a lot of years preaching the love of God to entitled and jaded American youth who had never worked for or deeply needed the love of God. They liked me, but that bore very little fruit in the long run. One must wait and yearn for grace to achieve its purpose. Cheap grace is not grace at all. I think this is why Jesus is presented as cursing the barren fig tree

(Matthew 21:19). Even God expects a return, a pass-through account, as it were. If not, it means the gift was not received at all. Authentic salvation, like love, has an effective quality to it. It works through you.

Initiation insisted on physical and concrete perform-ance and behavior. It is not a verbal exercise or a support group, where the ego can always say whatever it needs to say to get what it wants. This, in my opinion is the Achilles' heel of the present psychological, conversational model of enlightenment. In seminaries or any idealis-tic system, it creates a large number of submarines, who go underground until after ordination, licensing, or pro-motion. Ask anyone who does job interviews about the reliability of what people say during an interview or write on their resumes. We now look for a clear behavioral skill set that has been proven over time.

INITIATION AND COMMUNITY

From the initiate's perspective, membership in the group and loyalty to the group are valued and taken seriously—if they are worked for, invested in, and owned over a long period of time. The elders know that "from whom little is demanded, nothing can be expected." If it is a free lunch, it will be forgotten, rejected, or given away just as freely. Like Esau, we will sell our birthright for a "mess of pottage" (Genesis 25:34). Many of us are amazed at how easily so many young men have left priesthood, the vowed life, marriage, or a new job within a few months after commitment. One wonders if there is any loyalty to anything beyond the private self.

Therefore, the boy needs a valued group, a society, a community that he will be sent from, initiated by, and returned to. Without this home base to be accountable to, initiation is well nigh impossible. There are few such accountability systems today, which might be at the core of our problem. Even groups like Weight Watchers seem to understand this. There are some strong families, small groups, and healthy storefront churches that serve the same purpose.

The group believes for me when I can't, and it calls me to the next level if I can stay in there with them. It provides *an accountability system* that forces me out of my heady illusions and into concrete behavior. The single greatest weakness of most New Age systems and liberal churches is that there is no accountability system for what one says one believes, and as a result it changes from month to month, according to the whims of the ego, temperament, and social pressure. So-called conservative groups tend to last and produce things that last, although outsiders and liberals hate to admit it.

FATHER HUNGER

Even if our elders today do not have much initiatory wisdom to give, I can say that many men, and young men in particular, still want it. Father hunger is hard to talk about because it is one of the most vulnerable parts of a man, his desperate need for an older, wiser, or stronger man to guide him, believe in him, affirm him, concretely teach him, challenge him, and correct him. Men need men to keep their edges hot and clean, whereas women keep us warm and soft. Those are two different needs.

Men crave male attention at all ages but cannot openly ask for it. So they hang around other men at sports events, in bars, in Lions Clubs, at military academies, in wars, and at work sites, and hope that it will rub off somehow. It looks too much like weakness and neediness to name it consciously, so we garner male attention in all kinds of macho ways. As strong as the sexual drive is, and as beautiful as the company of women is, men all over the world create venues and situations where they can be together with other men, often in exclusive settings. It is a different energy entirely. Women are allowed the same, and take it, but for some reason they mistrust it in men.

In many men this male hunger has the shape of a full father wound, and sometimes I wonder if it is not the most common disability on this earth. I find it in every culture I visit, especially in those where the father is macho, distant, addicted, or emotionally unavailable.[45] Boys seem free to ask for what they need from their mothers; but boys secretly hope for what they need from their fathers. They curl up in their mom's lap even as young teenagers, but they have long stopped most body contact with Dad. From him, they need to know that he really wants to give them his attention and affection, without their asking. They love it when he takes the initiative, even though they won't always let on.

Boys seem to long for a kind of male mothering, which is a combination of fathers teaching them practical skills for success and survival, yet doing it with deliberate choice and personal desire. From Mom, they want the nesting, nurturing, talking, and listening. It is Dad's job, however, to lead us into the outer world and give us security and confidence beyond the nest. He needs to choose us — from the other children — and lead us into bigger worlds *with him.* For a child to have to enter the larger world unsupported and unguided by his father is a lifelong and gnawing sadness. I have heard the story too many times, and seen the nervous twitch on the mouth and in the eyes as the story is told, even in older men. They never forget.

The relationship between fathers and sons is too deep for words and touches upon primeval and foundational longing.[46] A son wants Dad to give him his male energy, and then he wants to know that he has something to give back to his father, almost as an equal. Why do you think playing catch is such a common memory for so many men? He does not just want to be on the receiving end. It is the mutual self-giving of father and son that creates Spirit, which is the basic metaphor for God in much of John's Gospel. Maybe love for our father is the first experience of power and influence in the life of another, for Mom is apparently experienced as an extension of "me," but Dad is the first "other" to come into my life: "If I can matter for him and to him, perhaps I will matter in the larger world!"

The male need for the male is in men's hardwiring, and most do not understand its depth or meaning, especially since it has taken so many unhealthy forms: blind obedience, unquestioned warfare, sick hierarchies, gender identity confusion, false dedication to bosses and companies, pedophile and punk relationships, sadomasochistic sex. Fortunately, father hunger is also acted out in healthier forms like bonding with a coach or mentor, joining the army, going to an all-male school, and general male roughhousing and camaraderie. We can see the adoring look on little boys as they watch older men work, play, fight, or just gesture, and their quick attempts at imitation. We can see teenage boys make nervous, stuttering attempts to talk to their heroes, in the powerful *senex-puer* connection.[47] I see father hunger in older men, when they talk to me as a priest or a teacher, often loving or even needing to turn to my title of Father. Numerous men have asked if they could use my title even after I told them to call me Richard. Sometimes they are older than me, but the secure, happy look on their face when they insist on using it makes me realize it has nothing to do with *me* and everything to do with the father hunger in their soul. My life is not about me.

For a blessing to be a blessing it must always come from one who is higher in some felt or real sense: an older man, a good man, a father figure, one with the energy of a king, one who has real power, one who gives what Dad could not or would not give. Much of the animal world seems to have this need for approval from the alpha male, and I am sure it partly explains the longevity of the divine right of kings and the power of the papacy; it also explains many peoples' rabid, irrational hatred of all male authority.

We seem to operate in an archetypal way for one another, quite apart from our actual personality. I remember how inauthentic I felt when I first raised my right hand as a twenty-seven-year-old new priest to bless a packed church; many of those in attendance were older than myself. Only later did I realize what words I was using. I was not speaking in my own name, but "in the name of the Father and of the Son." *I* was not blessing them. *I* had no power of my own with which to empower them, not at age twenty-seven, but I was somehow a channel, even more by doing it in magician's vestments and invoking archetypal titles of the Father and the Son! Religious transformation works best when you know you are an instrument and not the origin, an aqueduct and not the source. This is the basis for unbound personal self-confidence as a minister, but it is all based in confidence in another, not in just yourself.

Lovely companionship and conversation come from peers and equals, and this is very comforting; but true blessings come from fathers, who have already attained their mature manhood. In his poem entitled "Vacillation," William Butler Yeats captured the moment when he felt himself coming into that mature manhood. Note that the moment when he can receive the blessing is precisely when he knows he has the power to give it away. You have to be a son somewhere before you can be a generative father or a life-giving brother to someone else:

> My fiftieth year had come and gone,
> I sat a solitary man,
> In a crowded London shop,
> An open book and empty cup
> On the marble table-top.
>
> While on the shop and street I gazed
> My body of a sudden blazed;
> And twenty minutes more or less
> It seemed so great my happiness,
> That I was blessed and could bless.[48]

Nine

YOU ARE GOING TO DIE

The surprise of surprises is that although everybody who has ever lived in this world has died, for some reason, we think we won't.
— HINDU APHORISM

Death is not primarily a medical event. Death is a personal and spiritual event, yet we are largely concerned about preparing for the medical. — DR. IRA BYOCK

WHY ARE SO MANY thinking young men attracted today to very conservative politics and fundamentalist religion? Why do so many seek out things like strict military training, black-and-white answers, or some big theory to explain everything? Perhaps the more chaotic the time a young man grows up in, the more he will need order, authority, certitude, and some kind of overarching explanation for the world — in a word, tradition. Such a healthy respect for grounding is a sign of a solid and intelligent person, in my experience, yet it often becomes an end in itself. Why does something seemingly ancient have such power over so many men? And why do they try to construct it into such heroic projects for themselves? Is this not the story line of history?

Death, in any form, is the great human enemy. A man constructs much of his life to avoid it, to delay it, to deny it. He seeks to ground himself in something eternal, or at least lasting. To touch upon this seeming immortality, a man normally does two things. Looking backward he begins some kind of search for "firstness," according to Charles Sanders Peirce.[49] While looking forward he seeks to be a part of some kind of "heroic project," according to Ernest Becker.[50] These are the two classic male patterns for overcoming death and touching upon the eternal. Initiation addressed both of these temptations by making the young man face his death head on. It worked. It connected him with the heroic and energetic to send him into the future, but it also connected him with the ancient and the traditional to ground him in reality. Initiation provided a grounding wire and lightning rod at the same time. This is the conservative-radical tension you inevitably see in all healthy religion to this day. It is pure genius, and it was a young man's first experience of the sacred.

I will explain them both because, like most genius, it is very subtle. Authentic initiation gave the man some hint of "firstness," some experience of primary and ultimate grounding, some connection with the ancestors, the ancient, and the past. Charles Sanders Peirce describes it well: "Firstness is what the world was to Adam on the day he opened his eyes to it, before he had drawn any distinctions or had become conscious of himself....It is immediate, fresh, new, original, spontaneous, free, vivid, conscious and evanescent."[51] Firstness always feels like the sacred. It is the only way out of the endless questions that stir in our heads and make us tired, dizzy, and afraid, and I would say that, until a man has had a foundational sacred experience — some experience of firstness — he is basically adrift and eccentric. And he is terrified of death.

Somehow the initiation instinct realized that facing one's death was the ultimate encounter with the sacred. Ironically, walking through one's fear of the last thing became an encounter with the first thing, and a young man was then free to live, often for the first time outside of his head and his fear. Death encounters seem to be the primary way to build or rebuild a real life. Then life itself, in all its depth and beauty, becomes the unquestionable gift, the ultimate sacred. If we knew we were going to live forever and always had more chances, I doubt that we would ever grow up, search outside ourselves, or find the big picture.

Because death is very hard for youth to experience or know, most young men start by looking backward instead of forward. Most men and cultures start their spiritual search by looking for origins and foundations and ancient things. Such are the beginnings of most religions. Firstness, which feels like the sacred, becomes their guarantee of lastness, and even everlastingness. It explains the common idealization of the past and of ancient things; it is probably why people presume that religion must be conservative and traditional. (But they are only half right, as the prophets and Jesus make very clear!) This sacralization of the past is emblazoned in all the structures of patriarchy: royal families must pretend they go back to King Arthur or some saint, Americans have to mythologize George Washington and Thomas Jefferson, Roman Catholics look for some kind of proof of unbroken apostolic succession. Every cult is based on some kind of ancient hidden code or secret. We need blue blood once we find out that red blood dies. Religion and state go to great lengths to maintain these traditions and mythologies because if some final supreme court or sacred stone is missing, all we have is the endless vertigo and violence of imagination, competing egos, and competing claims, even within ourselves. There is no solid ground. There is no outer reference point to umpire our game. We are trapped in a senseless cultural whirlpool, while the soul and mind want an eternal rock.

In other words, we want eternal life but we substitute the old times instead. Finally the old times pass and show their negative sides, yet we re-create them in our idealized memory as a substitute for the eternal and as a shield against death. Please don't go there for long, brothers. It is just a starting place. Healthy religion always finds God in the present much more than in the past. *The past is only to create a runway for us so we have some communal assurance that ours is a valid experience.* The instinct for firstness is good and necessary, for in firstness a man knows that he has a home base and a starting line. The trouble is that many people spend their whole life defending and protecting their takeoff point.

Experiences of the ancient are often an aesthetic, mental, or sentimental substitute for the real living waters, but they can also be a premonition and an invitation to the greater picture. Educated people often prefer the aesthetic substitute of art and fine words (smells and bells religion), and the uneducated tend to prefer the sentimentality and certitudes of popular religion (religion as spectacle or reassurance); however, both can be substitutes for true transcendence and breakthrough. Ideally, once a man has touched upon authentic firstness, which is really to touch upon pure being, mere forms will no longer be anything more than that — forms and formulas, but not *the thing in itself.* The artistic, the moralistic,

the sentimental, the doctrinaire will no longer fully satisfy him. They are mere teases and signposts. He knows
his home base.

One could say that the entire Bible is about Adam seeking to return home to the garden where God first created
him and named him for the dust of the earth, *adamah*
(Genesis 2:7). God's last words to him were, "You came
from dust and unto dust you shall return" (Genesis 3:19).
But Adam gradually loses his fear of being dust, which
is to lose the fear of who he is. He forever knows what
God once did with dust! This supposed man of dust was
the chosen container for the very breath of God! Once he
stops separating and running and realizes that it is about
going back to where he started — and knowing it for the
first time — Adam returns. In the final book of the Bible,
humanity returns to the garden, as it were. There they are
fed from the masculine tree of life (Revelation 2:7) and
the feminine river of life (22:1), which has become the
city of God on earth (21:1–4). Heaven and earth are no
longer separate, and neither is Adam, and neither are we.

Strange, isn't it? We have to leave home and come back
home, fall and return. It is the classic pattern. "First the
fall, and then the recovery from the fall, and both are the
mercy of God," says Julian of Norwich. The man in all of
us who falls and fails, who *must* fall and *must* fail, is called
Adam; the man in all of us who gratefully returns, who
always says yes, is called Christ. The first, as Paul says, is
already "living soul," and the second is "life-giving spirit"
(1 Corinthians 15:45). Both are the work of God! Both are
in us. The only Christ we can be is the Christ that is first
and always Adam. Our divinity is precisely a fullness of
humanity, not a rejection or denial of it. Grace can only
build on nature, not deny it.

Remember that I said man looks forward too. He also tries to overcome death by being famous, strong, significant, remembered, smart, and superreligious. Every young man wants to somehow be a hero. You cannot take it away from him. As Ernest Becker brilliantly taught, all of men's heroic dramas are his attempt to stare down and overcome death. I would call his book *The Denial of Death,* which won the Pulitzer Prize for nonfiction in 1973, one of the foundational books that prepared me to write this book. The heroic instinct in males, according to Becker, is man's attempt to live forever. It is the source of his greatest creativity and courage, and God surely uses it. But it is also what Becker calls a "vital lie" —a lie that gives man energy, vitality, and direction, but only for a while, and eventually his heroics will and must fail him. Is this not the story line of half of the world's literature? It was also the subplot and message of every initiation rite.

WANDERLUST

The script of nearly every classic male story or fairy tale finds the hero traveling afar, but often wandering aimlessly and without a clear goal. If he does have a goal, it is never the real one. We perceive this desire to wander and travel in most men, almost as if exotic landscapes, different places, and new horizons will reveal to them their soul and their identity.[52] The Germans, who always seem to have great words for things, call it "wanderlust." The goal is always elsewhere; anywhere but here will show me my truth, the male imagines.

Many men of my generation joined the navy to see the world; others of us joined the Franciscans for similar reasons. Black men in the 1960s looked to the Nation of Islam or to the King of Ethiopia to find their roots. Roman Catholics tend to idealize the faceless, distant saints of medieval shrines. They need know nothing at all about the saint's actual life, just a name and a place; their imagination will spin whatever web of meaning it needs. Young men like to backpack into places where no one has ever been before.

Today young men are fascinated by journeys to Tibet or Bali, by old Latin Masses, rapture theories, extraterrestrials, dinosaurs, Renaissance fairs, Civil War enactments, any imagined America of their grandfathers. Such longing and nostalgia is probably inspired by the fear that the ordinary, the here and now, could never be sufficient. We long for distant absolutes, perhaps seeking a confirmation of the absolute we already intuit within ourselves. Like Jacob we eventually awake from our sleep and say, "God was in this place, and I never knew it!" (Genesis 28:16). But in the first half of life, the big truth is always elsewhere and out there. Remember, we have to leave before we can come back.

One form that this leaving takes is for the young man to return to the natural, to his roots and beginnings, to be Adam naked in the garden, to feel himself and the world around him fresh and unspoiled, with no barriers or fear. I am often struck by how many men do their solitude time during the initiation rites buck naked, even though I never tell them to. Men frequently have a strong dissatisfaction with all things artificial, manufactured, or plastic. Most men like to be outside and in nature.

The most common location for religious experience for males, even in the Bible, is in nature. Note that neither

Abraham, Moses, Jacob, Job, Jonah, Elijah, nor Jesus have their great experiences in the temple or in any formal sacred space! This is very telling. Anything too pretty, organized, and nice gnaws away at the male soul; the male craves contact with the substantial, the solid, the authentic, the eternal, which seems virile to him. He prefers leather to lace, and stone to linoleum. And very often, dirt to cleanliness! These qualities feel more honest and true to the male.

What man is not filled with awe before ruins and artifacts, ancient caves or carvings, arrowheads or pottery, exploring and discovering undiscovered places? Is there a boy who does not dream of such things? I would say this is a search for ourselves, our ancient soul, our origins, our uncluttered originality in God, our own immaculate conception. As the Zen masters say, "The face you had before you were born." If that discovery does not happen on some level, religion has little ability to broker and guide one's journey because all spiritual cognition is really recognition.

That split between doctrine and life, words and personal experience, probably explains the rather high incidence of atheism in the West recently. I am told that statistically, the only group larger than Roman Catholics in America is *former* Roman Catholics! They are very often the disillusioned idealists who were given the right words and rituals, but never the actual experience, so they throw out the baby with the bathwater in their bitter disappointment. Like poor lovers, we flirt with people, we tease and seduce them, but we do not make love to them. Most former Christians I meet are not bad people, just *inexperienced* people.

What men want and need is what the great religious traditions have promised them: an experience that knocks on the hard bottom of life and death. As D. H. Lawrence said, "The world fears a new experience more than it fears anything. Because a new experience displaces so many old experiences. And it is like trying to use muscles that have perhaps never been used, or that have been going stiff for ages. It hurts horribly. The world doesn't fear a new idea. It can pigeon-hole any idea. But it can't pigeon-hole a real new experience. It can only dodge. The world is a great dodger, and the Americans the greatest. Because they dodge their own very selves."[53] Thus the rites of passage were exactly that—ritual experience—and not discussions of ideas, debates, or logical argumentation. Neither were rites of passage therapeutic discussions or problem-solving sessions, which is the most common mistake of people who try to manufacture a quick initiation rite. They turn it into a psychological or personal growth experience, when *it is primarily a cosmology, an epiphany, and a death experience.* It is always set in the context of a journey, alone and in nature, where all the truths can be revealed.

It seems you are not ready to die until you have once truly lived. People who touch upon real life are ironically the ones who can also let go of it. It is people who have not yet begun to live who fear death. They know true insight has not happened to them yet, which leaves them without a center, foundation, or even primal desire. They have no *eros* or élan vital. Their core has not been touched and so they have nothing to harken back to or look forward to or anything to trust deeply within. They did not experience a firstness, so lastness feels scary, impossible, and almost unthinkable. They are afraid. This is most of humanity.

RITUALS OF DEATH

Initiation evokes the sacred and is the primary means of making us human and giving death a positive value.

— MIRCEA ELIADE

Since it was absolutely central that a man die before he dies, every initiation rite I studied had created some ritual and even theatrical way in which a man could walk through that scary threshold in symbolic form. They could not experience rebirth, being born again, without experiencing some real form of death first. The old self always has to die before the new self can be born, which is the passover experience that we resist. In the language of mystery religions and John's Gospel (12:24), "The grain of wheat had to die or it remained just a grain of wheat— but if it died, it would bear much fruit." There it all is in one jam-packed and hard-to-swallow pill.

Sometimes the initiate was sent alone, away from his tribe, for an extended period, which was tantamount to psychic death. Sometimes he had to fast (for forty days and forty nights) to let his body begin to die. Almost always, there were various and extended trials in which he had to risk failure, actual death, danger, and fear. Always, his comfortable self-image as his mother's boy had to be stripped from him, and all other badges of identity were taken away in his extended status as a novice, a ghost, a dead man, a man of no account, a man who could not speak or be spoken to, a man of neither upper nor lower class, a man with no name. This took him back to a state of being a useless child, who Jesus said is the only one who can get it. Any social roles or proficiencies that he had acquired meant nothing, and any special clothing was taken away.

Most, if not all, of the initiation was done in various forms of undress. The young man's psyche and identity were almost stripped bare so the rebuilding and rebirthing could begin and the past could be put behind him in a definitive way. He often buried some symbol of his boyhood in the forest and walked away from it. We have no comparable teaching structure today, except the sufferings that life itself extends to us, but then it often does not feel like sacred space when it happens. It feels like merely an unfortunate accident — which we need to fix or change.

The genius of our ancestors was that they exposed and revealed pain in a sacred space, which makes all the difference in the world. They were psychodrama geniuses! Now pain is no longer a scary unknown, an unfortunate mistake, something we must change, but maybe an entranceway! I suspect that is why Catholics need to present a crucifix at the center of the sanctuary. The crucified man is not so much a religious logo as it is the soul's logic. As Eckhart Tolle says, "You do not need to be a Christian to understand the deep universal truth that is contained in symbolic form in the image of the cross."[54] Before such transformative images, worst things can become best things. It is an ultimate juxtaposition, and it allows us to call a murderous failure the redemption of the world!

Inside the sacred space of initiation, there were invariably ritual enactments like drowning, dipping, burying, entrance into one's tomb, all of which came together in the Pauline notion of baptism (see Romans 6:3–11). Men lay naked on the earth in the ashes, which is remembered with ashes on foreheads on Ash Wednesday. There were sacred whippings and anointings for death and burial, which became the symbolic slap and oil of Confirmation. The old Benedictines used to lie prostrate before the altar at their final vow ceremony, the funeral pall and candles placed over them, while parts of the requiem Mass were sung over their "dead" bodies. This is no surprise because they are the only Order old enough to have had contact with the historic initiation rites of Europe.

In every case, some ritual of death—and resurrection—was the centerpiece of all male initiation. It is probably why Jesus sought out and submitted to this offbeat death and rebirth ritual of John the Baptist down by the riverside, when his own temple had become more concerned with purity codes than transformation. It is probably why he kept talking to his disciples, three times in Mark's Gospel, about the necessity of this death journey, and why three times they changed the subject (8:31–10:45). It is undoubtedly why he finally stopped talking about it, and just did it, not ritually but really. It is why death and resurrection, the paschal mystery, is the only theme of every single Eucharist no matter what the feast or season. It takes us that many years and seasons to overcome our resistance to death.

The transformational journey of death and resurrection is the only—big and always denied—message. It really is the way we are saved, even though many now find the language a bit embarrassing. For some reason, we are content with our unhappiness and our solitude, and we punctuate it with polite worship services, which is good for keeping us in correct alignment. Yet Jesus did not once tell us to *worship* him; he only told us to *follow* him on this necessary three-day journey. And by the way, "three days" did not necessarily mean Friday to Sunday. It was a classic initiatory phrase for going the distance or the full cycle!

Sometimes the rituals themselves had a strong quality of disillusionment, so the initiate would never confuse the ritual with the necessary and painful reality of death. This sounds very risky, I am sure, but when I see what Catholics have done with the Mass and what Protestants have done with the Bible, I recognize how easy it is to make the medium the message. Catholics go to Mass repeatedly since we are slow learners and slow transformers, but Jesus did it only once. Protestants argue about the Bible, doctrines, and moralisms instead of following Jesus into new and risky places. The new para-churches love religious entertainment instead of loving peace or justice. Warlike heads of state can normally be assured of Christians' total support — all in poor Jesus's name. We all prefer our rituals to anything real or risky. Without some kind of disillusionment of forms, religion invariably becomes idolatry of forms. Ritual is risky business and religion is dangerous business, so I will devote a section to this classic corrective of initiation rites.

RITUAL DISENCHANTMENT

The best things cannot be talked about. The second best things are almost always misunderstood. So we spend our lives talking about the third best things.   — HEINRICH ZIMMER

For some reason, initiations often included (not always) what we call ritual disenchantment, intended to free the initiate from a false idolatry of the religious symbols themselves. Most human beings cling to new spiritual symbols in literal ways, and this is understandable. But unfortunately they gradually let the symbol stand over and above the reality. That is the very meaning of a superstition (*super-stare*, "to stand above"). A new encounter with the Holy is harder to maintain than a relationship with objects, words, and totems. We prefer the familiar, and God is never totally familiar, but always new. "He is wild, you know!" C. S. Lewis said. It is easier to hold a sacred object, return to a memorable place, or mimic transformative words than to trust and rely on the new life. Many people like religion. Most fear the mutuality of presence. Jesus offered us himself more than any moral conclusions or ritual practice. The biblical revelation is the revelation of an utterly engaging presence, as Vatican Council II declared. God is revealing God's self,[55] not theological statements that we can be right about. Mutual presence feeds the soul. Propositions feed the mind's need for control and the ego's need for satisfaction.

Wise teachers and traditions unlock the whole thing from inside to create a natural corrective to idolatry: Moses breaks the tablets of the law at the foot of the mountain, Isaiah and Jeremiah make fun of cultic religion, Jesus overthrows tables inside the temple, the real identity of kachinas is revealed to Pueblo children, the sacred initiators take off their masks and often abuse the boys verbally and physically (but all ritually inside sacred space, which changes the chemistry of the act). In less dramatic form, even our formal religious rituals today have some built-in disillusionment. Taking off religious vestments after Mass, blowing out the candles, deconsecrations, laicizations, annulments, dispensations—all say that the holy can revert to unholy, so be careful what you worship as divine or forever. Bell, book, and candle were ceremoniously taken away from the defrocked priest.

Thanks to the caricatures of political cartoonists, our daily newspapers present regular ritual disenchantments of our heads of state or anybody pretentious or pompous.

There seems to be a need to pull back the curtain so we can see that the great and powerful Wizard of Oz is actually, simply, a mortal man like you and me. It is supposed to be both a relief and a promise, although many people, unfortunately, just become cynical and angry about all wizards. Don't waste your time doing that. You will miss the point.

Humor is also a major form of ritual disenchantment. The Pueblo clowns mock and laugh at evil, Islam laughs at the Haj, and numerous Asian rituals spoof significant entities. The devil must be laughed at and robbed of his numinous character or we end up worshiping evil, death, and obscenity as if it were larger than life. That is what has happened in Satanism and some forms of heavy metal music. If you do not show the limited scope of things like religious ritual, sexual ritual, and the power of evil, they tend to become demigods, or what the Bible would call idols or golden calves. You must not give them too much power or they possess you. An ability to laugh at evil and relativize symbols—without dismissing them— is usually a sign of a rather healthy person. Puritans and reformers can't laugh. Old nuns who worked in the jails with me could laugh with the prostitutes and joke with the johns. A holy old priest here in New Mexico refills the holy dirt at the healing sanctuary of Chimayo—from a pile of dirt behind the church—with no apology or needed explanation. He knows it is not the dirt that heals!

A certain kind of ritual disenchantment is not helpful just for individuals; it is also necessary for a religion and state to grow up. Without such disenchantment, it is more or less inevitable that most social institutions will become imperialistic, self-worshiping, self-maintaining, and almost catatonic in their repetition of words, rituals, and symbols. I thought we Catholics were alone in this until I attended my first American Legion gathering with an uncle, and again when I lived in a Buddhist monastery in Japan.[56]

Zadok, Annas, Caiaphas, and the Pharisees represent a priestly commitment to the ritual system as an end in itself. By contrast, the prophets, Isaiah, Jeremiah, Amos, Hosea, John the Baptist; and Jesus were always relativizing the forms to point us toward the substance. Judaism is archetypal religion. It retains the classic symbols and names for both sides—how to do it wrong and how to do it absolutely right. In effect, the Jewish prophets say that all forms and rituals are merely fingers pointing to the moon, and occasionally the forms have to get out of the way so we can actually see the moon. (See, for example, Isaiah 1:11–18, Jeremiah 7:4–15, and much of Amos.)

The prophets of Israel turned ritual disenchantment and God enchantment into their major job description. It's amazing that there is almost no room for such people in conservative Judaism, mainline Catholicism, or Evangelical Protestantism today, groups that think of themselves as quite traditional and orthodox. We seem to like the mystification that ritual provides, no matter what the prophets said or the tradition taught. Many young Catholic priests are returning to a very cultic notion of priesthood over any notion of servant leadership. One knows they have not been initiated.

Ten

WHAT IS THE SHAPE OF THE MALE SOUL?

Four Mighty Ones are in every man.
— WILLIAM BLAKE, *THE FOUR ZOAS*

DESPITE THE RECENT SEARCH for unisex everything, despite feminist denials, despite the anger at maleness in recent decades, despite men's doubts about themselves, the grand nature of the male soul is self-evident. We like it, we fear it, we disseminate it, we push against it, we love it, we take it for granted. Like love itself, and like the female soul, it makes the world go round. So much so that languages, which reveal the basic mind structure, often have masculine and feminine forms. It is probably the ultimate template and archetype for the structuring of the universe. It is at least half of all of us, and half of everything, even insects, mammals, flowers, and electric sockets.

Many people are so angry at patriarchy, or false male power, that it makes them afraid to recognize the good power and the good passion of men. We have all found life and love at the male banquet. Maleness is half of the mystery of God, and if we do not enjoy it, we are missing out on something "very good" (Genesis 1:31), at least half of who we are, whether we are a man or a woman.

Researchers Robert Moore and Doug Gillette have found that the characters in male legend, myth, story—the universal images that attract men—invariably circle around four constellating images, which some call archetypes or ruling images.[57] Images of a king, a warrior, a lover, and a magician or wise man seem to be four parts of every man, his primary fascinations, the major quadrants of his soul, if you will. They challenge him, they fascinate him, they threaten him, and he seems unable to totally ignore them. He often overidentifies with one of them, which invariably takes on its dark and compulsive side, but the mature man honors and integrates all four parts of his soul. They seem to naturally balance and regulate one another, and they make a man both whole and holy. It could be called the very shape of male holiness.

People have questioned this seeming oversimplification of maleness into a mere four aspects, and many other possible archetypes, like the divine child, the rebel, the holy fool, or the wanderer, are put forth. But as I work with these, they invariably can be classed as stages, variations, or negative aspects of one of the big four.

On men's retreats we have often taken a Gospel and noted when Jesus operates like a warrior, when he operates like a sage, when like a lover, and when like a king. It makes a great template for ongoing conversion. Honestly, Jesus is amazingly integrated, even by contemporary psychological standards; all four male archetypes are clearly represented in him, and very often in dramatic form. You can even see how his lover balances his warrior, his magician informs his king, his king tempers his warrior, and so on. Jesus walks firmly on a high-wire of male integrity, and you don't have to be a Christian to appreciate that.[58]

JESUS AS A WARRIOR

Let's start with the warrior archetype, since that is where most young men start and are first fascinated. Jesus's frequent use of the apocalyptic language of the prophets, his aggressive stand against human suffering, his unapologetic battle with evil, sickness, and political and religious oppression, his non-whining directness about his task and call, his ability to toughen himself alone in the desert, his identification with good power but nonetheless power — all of these show Jesus to be a very defined warrior. "I have not come to bring peace but a sword" (Matthew 19:34) shows that he is not afraid of power, especially the more courageous power of nonviolence, which, as Martin Luther King said, "is not for cowards." Jesus speaks of the sword, but then he utterly redefines it on his own terms.

Jesus took on the religious establishment and did not back down before the Roman occupiers. His good warrior is clearly revealed in his lack of need for enemies and in his freedom to forgive them. He made it his life's work to protect the true boundaries of his Jewish religion, but he did not bother to protect the boundaries of his country, which is rather telling. He is just as at home in Tyre, Sidon, and Gentile territory as in Jerusalem. He refused to answer phony or disingenuous questions, he staged a demonstration in the temple against his own religion, he was able to drink the cup in Gethsemane, he faced his night of torture, and, of course, he bore his flagellation, humiliation, and cross. He knew how to defend himself and those who were defenseless, the poor, handicapped, and marginalized. His ability to endure his death with total dignity and freedom reveals a warrior of the first magnitude. This is the part of Jesus that Mel Gibson's movie, *Passion,* shows us, probably because it is the most idealized part of Gibson himself. We tend to see ourselves everywhere, and Jesus has served in this way as a kind of lure to lead and develop the soul; he confirms the good parts of our manhood and then leads us beyond them to the full shape of holiness.

Jesus turned passive resistance into an art form by largely ignoring the Romans, which is the ultimate negation of false power. There is no indication that he ever took the short walk down the road to Sepphoris, the Roman colony very close to his hometown of Nazareth. He fought good and needed controversies, but he picked his controversies wisely. He could be silent, leave, or change the question, when he saw confrontation was useless. His inner warrior was as secure as his outer one. Jesus was no soft New Age guy, which is why some liberals have trouble with him. As mentioned earlier, Jesus described God's love as conditional, demanding, and expectant, which is a very male and warrior way of loving.

JESUS AS A WISE MAN

Jesus did two things in his daily ministry: preach and heal, heal and preach, and the healings usually illustrated the themes of his preaching, while the preaching justified and amplified the meaning of the healing. Jesus sooner or later illustrates most of the names and faces of the magician archetype: boy wonder or divine child, agent of transformation, master of initiation, mentor, spiritual director, truth speaker, social critic, father confessor (which is a combination of king and magus), prophet (which is a combination of warrior and magus), and mystic (which is a combination of lover and magus). His teaching had enough natural authority to move people to leave everything and to be willing to die for him. To speak with authority is a combination of king and wise man. Jesus's frequent use of what we would now call mystical language — riddles, parables, aphorisms, messages from another world, "I and the Father are One" language, speaking with calm certitude in the name of God—put Jesus in a category all his own.

It is no surprise that the West chose him as its primary magician, teacher, and wise man. Unfortunately, we have tended to make him give us quick and final answers more than teaching us journey and process. We have demanded "what" from him, when as all wise men, he is primarily teaching "how." He only directly answers *three* of the 183 questions that are asked of him in the four Gospels! (Yet we made his followers into "answer men"!) The ego prefers kings to wise men, answer-givers over spiritual guides, *potestas* (dominative power) over *auctoritas* (inner authority). We even made the magi into three kings, although there is not a speck of evidence to justify that switch in the text. That's how much we fear wise men, and it serves as evidence of the breadth of criticism that they normally bear. The prophet would be the highest form of the magician, and I have never found a church in all the world named Jesus the Prophet, while thousands are named Christ the King. That's how much we fear prophets, a title that Jesus never rejected or denied.

JESUS AS A LOVER

Probably this is what we like and remember most about Jesus because it is what we most desire from God. Jesus is compassionate, forgiving, accepting, nurturing — and rule-breaking for people who are the same. He is clearly connected to his heart and his emotions, and the text speaks of a man of great empathy and sympathy. "Sighs that came from deep within," weeping over missed opportunities, feeling "from his very bowels," and showing "compassion for the crowds" are phrases used of a divine one, who is usually above mundane passions and feelings. His ability to enjoy is less attested to, except for his kindly observations on nature, flowers, birds, and the simple work patterns of ordinary people. His investment in people's lives and his commitment to alleviate their pain is his very soul. He could clearly bond with people at a deep level and personally care for their urgent needs and even their wants and desires. He never once appears to be anal-retentive, emotionally repressed, or any kind of puritan altar boy.

The foundational meaning of his healing ministry is that Jesus—and God by implication—does not like human suffering and is willing to alleviate it whenever possible. I assume he danced at Cana, and he was surely not afraid of intoxicating wine if he produced 150 gallons at the end of the party (Baptists beware!). His farewell discourse and foot washing at the Last Supper speak of a tender, sympathetic, and tactile kind of man. His surrender and forgiveness on the cross stands as the deepest archetype of sacrificial love in the Western psyche. There is no indication of a repressed, split, or withheld kind of life. He was *eros, philia, storge,* and *agape* (the four Greek words for love) all in one person at different times. It is surely Jesus as the consummate and compassionate lover that has captured the world's imagination, even that of non-Christians.

JESUS AS A KING

If the king archetype means the man who holds the big picture together, then it is no surprise that Jesus's number-one preaching theme is the Kingdom of God. He always presents the biggest frame and the final perspective. The crowds' adoration and amassing seem to say that he exuded a larger-than-life persona, yet his very avoidance of fame, power, and messianic claims says that he was an inner king, and he did not need the trappings. "Mine is not a kingdom of this world," he says to the dark king, Pilate, but then he soon says, "I am a king" (John 18:37) and defines kingship as "bearing witness to the truth." The notice fixed to the cross is the final irony; "Jesus of Nazareth, King of the Jews" is a title for him that the Jews rejected, but they are merely the stand-ins for all of us, who all reject power over us. His kingship, precisely because it is so broad and so total, is doomed to be rejected by anybody who is still into tribalism and "belonging systems." We don't really like the big kingdom if it gets in the way of our smaller kingdoms—and it always does.

Do remember that the king is simply another name for the father or the grandfather, the paterfamilias, that strong and stable energy that can hold together chaos, fear, and doubt to an amazing degree, just as the queen does in feminine form. When Daddy is home, the house is safe and secure, psychologically and physically. When Jesus enters the room, people are healed, reconciled, and their devils flee. That is the power of the good father and the good king.

Of course, Jesus is not a king in any usual sense, but in the sense of the ultimate whole man, the man who holds warrior, wise man, and lover together in a lovely balance and symmetry. We end up rightly imaging him as the King of Kings, the Christ archetype, which is the archetype of wholeness, inclusion of the opposite, and forgiveness of the opponent. The King/Father is the oneness of God, which holds together all our disparate, divided, and inimical parts. A God who holds together everything, absolutely everything, is perhaps the deepest and truest meaning of monotheism. It is strange that the three monotheistic religions cannot operate this way. If there is one God, there is finally one reality. The king by his very connection to being says that everything belongs, and he invites everything to belong through forgiveness and mercy. He is the lightning rod that holds and passes the energy between heaven and earth, and pays the price for it through the darts and arrows of smaller men.

Interestingly enough, the church's ancient baptismal rite still uses these words as the candidate is anointed with sacred perfumed oil: "As Christ was anointed priest, prophet, and king, so may you live always as a member of his body." Priest is a form of the magician, prophet is a form of the warrior, the sacramental sensuality of sweet-smelling chrism covering the body is the touch and anointing of the lover—and they all come together in the promise of kingship, which is to say, wholeness. It is wholeness and holiness that we promise the initiate at baptism by anointing him as king.

Full archetypal manhood can be participated in only collectively. Note that the formula says, "as a member of his body." Don't ever put the burden of private perfect wholeness on yourself as an individual. That promise, appealing to the ego, has seduced and destroyed many religious people. Our wholeness comes from our related-ness to the king, which relieves any burden of being a king by ourselves. In full Christian initiation, we are promised some participation in male fullness, modeled and offered by Jesus as the "firstborn son" of all creation (see Colossians 1:15–20). But we are "heirs as well, heirs of God, and coheirs with Christ," as Paul loves to say (Romans 8:17). *It is about participation, not attainment.*

It is a holographic universe, and each fragment seems to mirror the whole and find its meaning there.[59] I guess Christians would call Jesus the ultimate hologram of what is going on in the universe. But we are holograms too — only a part, and yet genuine parts of the great whole. We called it salvation, but it soon became individualized and lost all its authenticity. The authentic goal of Christian initiation was to actually lead people to "share in the divine nature" (2 Peter 1:4). We have been faint to believe in such glory, even though that is the whole point! Only the Eastern Church dared to speak of divinization, while the West, Catholic and Protestant, made it into a laborious process of private heroism, at which few could succeed.

Life, Jesus tells us, is a participatory event, much more than any kind of achievement, obstacle course, or act of existential heroism. That is more the religion of the Greek God Zeus, instead of Jesus. It is not surprising that Latin translated God as *Deus* after Zeus, which soon became some form of *Dios* in all the Latin languages. This is precisely the kind of monarch that a trinitarian God is not, but it is what happens to a king when he is not also a good warrior, a wise sage, and a passionate lover. The God that Jesus wanted to introduce us to was so much more than Zeus!

INCLUDING AND NAMING THE NEGATIVE

Anything held up to the light will itself become light.
— EPHESIANS 5:14

I think it is very important to understand the unique nature of the male psyche and why male stories always need to have villains and bad guys, and even violence. It is important at this point to work with both sides of the male soul, revealing the negative and calling forth the positive—and the graced relationship between those two.

For some reason, most people think that religion should only be about the positive—healing, helping, and hoping. But my assumption is the opposite: *the way to transmute the pain of life is to reveal the wounded side of all things, and then place the wound inside sacred space.* Thus the biblical revelation is filled with stories of wars, massacres, adulteries, betrayals, rapes, injustice, and dishonesty. Much of it is not pretty or inspiring. It is about naming, facing, and forgiving the wounds of history, which is quite different than excluding them, denying them, or making them impossible. The Bible is honest theater and healing drama. It leaves the whole drama on stage for observation and critique.

The deliberate inclusion of the negative is the very meaning of the crucifixion, but there are constant examples throughout Jesus's life too. One simple example is when Jesus gratuitously insults a woman, but then he apologizes and strongly affirms her (Mark 7:24–30). How could Jesus be so imperfect? Purists don't know how to preach on the text, and they try to explain it away somehow. For pious types, this passage is not seemly, inspiring, or holy. Many Catholics in the past and New Agers today just refuse to read the Scriptures because it so obviously includes disappointing elements. (I did not like the Bible as a young man. Lives of the saints were much more inspiring.) The biblical revelation is not as uplifting as an exultant praise and worship service, a clear book on the success habits of highly effective people, a Mozart Mass, a circle dance, or a sweet May Crowning. But the Bible taught me that goodness, for humans, is a mistake overcome rather than the perfect avoidance of all mistakes.

We have confused the perfect with the good. We have confused God with humanity. God alone is perfect; we can merely participate in small doses, which is called goodness. This false search for the perfect, which only applies to God and maybe accounting, is a great disguise for egotism. It has often become a true enemy to the only good that is available to us, which is a truly wonderful but partial good. We do not want to live in a human world, it seems. We do not want to be a part, but the whole. Like Adam, we want to be "like gods" (Genesis 3:6). What pleases God, it seems, is not the perfection of the gift, but the willingness to give the gift, imperfect though it is. (Exactly as we would do with our own children.)

As Goethe realized, the seductive temptation that drives Faust into hell is the desire to create and maintain a utopian world of perfect people. It is the ultimate spiritual temptation. It looks so good and right, but it forces you to use and misuse power, which even God does not do. The same is true of J. R. R. Tolkein's *The Lord of the Rings.* The temptation is to try to enforce "the good" by dominative means—which then themselves become evil, which is exactly the lie of both fascism and communism. The movies never understood that subtlety.

We must live our lives in a painful cauldron of transformation, inside a mixed blessing, not in any enforced utopia. We are a mass of contradictions longing to be reconciled. We must live with the wound and learn from the wound, until it becomes our sacred wound. I remember the shock of being in a Spanish art museum and seeing a full-size painting of a wounded body of Jesus ascending into heaven. I finally got it! Heaven is not for angels at all, but for the wounded ones.

Good liturgy and good religion know that you must bring the whole story on full stage. Only then can you reveal and relate honestly to the full field of both weeds and wheat (Matthew 13:29), and only then will you stop being naïve about evil and projecting it elsewhere. "Let them both grow together until the harvest," Jesus said, and then God will take care of it. When you can be honest about the negative side of things, you can then reveal the good side—the good is then credible, powerful, and even more attractive and proceeds from freedom. That's why almost all drama has to have both heroes and villains, so they can play off of one another and also create one another. This is brilliantly presented in Stephen Schwartz's script and musical *The Wicked.*

Denying or hating the negative never makes it go away. You never resolve a problem by merely condemning it, personally or institutionally. That is not transformation but domination, and we typically confuse the two. You cannot contain evil by shaming it, but only by revealing it for what it is and then seeing the good as better. Salvation is sin forgiven much more than sin avoided. Couples begin to love only after their first fight and reconciliation. A man who owns his limitations and weeps over his sin is much more effective than one who thinks he has neither.

Is that not the very training of Peter, and then Paul? How
do we keep missing the obvious? I think it has something
to do with our dualistic mind and the oppositional nature
of the ego.

Here in New Mexico, our Pueblo peoples have created
both clowns and kachinas to expose the dark and light
side of things. There is the image of the good mother,
the Corn Maiden with blessings in both hands. But she is
balanced by the bad mother, the Ogre Woman with cas-
trating knife, mocking tongue, and whipping reeds. The
good father, the Sunface, mirrors your own radiance and
also holds blessings in both hands. But he is counterpoised
with the ugly-faced Ogre who mutilates you, humiliates
you, and beats you. The bad mother and father are ritually presented so we will not be unduly surprised or
shocked when they show themselves in real life. We will
know how to relate to badness instead of being trapped
inside it. The Pueblo clown ("Koshare") function is much
the same. He exposes and mocks the tribe's recent failings
publicly, like the year when I saw them wearing long bal-
loons like phalluses, rudely poking everybody. When the
negative presence is revealed, false innocence is denied
you, and true victory is offered.

The Far East did the same thing with dragons, mocking faces, and monsters who guard almost every door in
Africa, Asia, and Oceania. Westerners wonder why they
have so many ugly figures right at an entrance, and not
more smiley faces. We would prefer a waving Mickey
Mouse or a sentimental blond angel. The aggressive face
has something necessary and good to teach you about
the difficult and demanding side of things, about naiveté,
containment, perseverance, and your ability to stare evil
down. Don't confuse the negative with the hostile; they

are not the same. The negative is contained inside the truly positive; the hostile needs to be hostile and oppositional. Hostile people are never helpful; critics are necessary. Americans in particular tend to be trapped inside a happy-happy script and cannot easily integrate the negative. We want happy endings, and we would prefer the whole thing to be nice. It ends up nice, but not true.

If we want men to be nonviolent, humanized, and self-controlled, then it does little good to just keep railing against each of these problems. Show me where condemnation of anything has worked in the long haul, especially with men. In fact, we could make the case that it only increases their attraction and addiction. Can anyone honestly say that Christian countries are any less greedy, materialistic, or superficial than the other countries of the world? I have been pickpocketed only twice, both times in Catholic countries, Italy and the Philippines. I felt totally safe in India. There is some strange psychic appeal to forbidden fruit, which is revealed in the Adam and Eve story and many other fables and fairy tales too.

Paul says the same in an amazingly contemporary understanding of the perverse nature of the human person. He says that commands become temptations for human beings, and much of their attraction comes precisely from there being a law against them (Romans 7:7–8). He does not say to throw out the law, nor do I, but the most the law can do is try to name our sins; it is powerless to give spiritual strength. It gives information, not transformation. When my dark secret can be truthfully named in the sacred space of confession, it is no longer so dark or so attractive. We start the Mass with public confession, sort of like an AA meeting: "Hi, I'm Richard and

I am a sinner. Lord, have mercy." Now the gathering is correctly named—a gathering of needy sinners.

Anything idealized as totally good, other than the divinity itself, leads to idolatry of it, false expectation from it, and then disappointment and a false sense of betrayal when we see the truth. Even from our wife or friends. Anything seen as totally bad allows us to give it far too much power over us and against us. We then take on the same dark power to overcome it and become a mirror image of what we hate. That is the first principle of nonviolence. Jesus would call it trying to "drive out the devil by the prince of devils," and it never works in the end, but only continues the problem. The second evil is just as bad as the first, but for some reason we can't see the second evil. "Their bombs are bad but our bombs are good," we think, and no advancement is made beyond the morality of two children fighting in the backseat of a car. "She hit me first!" Like Jesus, we must absorb and transform the negative rather than replicate it through imitation. It is the only true resurrection and our only future.

Eleven

THE FOUR INITIATIONS

There is a basic wisdom that can help solve the world's problems. This wisdom does not belong to any one culture or religion, nor does it come only from the West or the East. Rather, it is a tradition of human warriorship that has existed in many cultures at many times throughout history.

— CHOGYAM TRUNGPA, *SHAMBHALA: THE SACRED PATH OF THE WARRIOR*

A truly spiritual and wise initiation must somehow address and initiate all four parts of a man's soul. Although I have spoken strongly in favor of ancient initiations, I must admit that only one or another part of a man was affirmed in most cultures, usually the warrior and perhaps some form of the magician. The king, or whole man, did emerge in the general population but rarely and then only toward the end of the man's life. The lover was either marginalized as a mere entertainer or artist, or he was assumed to be present in all men as a sexual person, but sexual does not necessarily mean lover, as we know. Celibacy in Buddhism, Hinduism, and Catholicism were undoubtedly attempts to educate and discipline the lover archetype. Our job today is much more difficult because we must affirm, educate, and validate *all four archetypes* and let them simmer and grow together to create a full man. Now we need enlightened and transformed magicians, lovers of life and beauty, and strong nonviolent warriors to produce truly big-picture men—or kings.

THE WARRIOR

IT SEEMS YOU CANNOT take the testosterone out of men, nor should you want to. We must honor male passion, the good warrior, and tame it for the common good and for larger purposes than mere tribal jingoism and group security. Liberals generally do not understand the good and necessary meaning of the warrior; while conservatives seem to presume that they *are* the civilized and humane warriors. The East has initiated the warrior with aikido, jujitsu, judo, karate, and the training of the noble Samurai.[60] We understood it and followed suit for a while with the initiation of the Christian knight, until it was brutalized and corrupted by the Crusades and internecine European wars. We totally destroyed any notion of the religious warrior during the Spanish and Roman Inquisitions, the religious wars of the Reformation, and the blessing of wars ever since. We abdicated our role of training the warrior, and now we end up with sacralized violence at many levels of our society, sadistically torturing prisoners, and brutalizing soldiers who cannot reenter polite society.

Martin of Tours, Francis of Assisi, Ignatius of Loyola, and Charles de Foucauld never stopped being knights and soldiers. They found the true and universal meaning of the warrior. They discovered the dark side of their warrior and learned from it, but they did not totally reject it. They sublimated it and consecrated it. The warrior archetype must be named and rightly initiated or he remains petty, violent, and unaccountable to self or society. If you don't work with it, it works against you. The young male takes pride in being taught discipline, focus, respect, boundaries, and self-denial. He knows he needs it, yet he also knows it has to be forced upon him because he will seldom seek it out by himself. I find that men understand this, even while they resist it.

Most male initiation rites had the boy do things like roll in ashes, cover himself with mud, dance very aggressively with violent gestures, strip and expose himself to the elements and to pain, mutilate his penis or other body parts, and wear dung in his hair. The male has to enact his aggressiveness and recognize how far it can lead him. He has to know the difference between good anger and egocentric rage. He has to taste oppositions' many layers and meanings and sense its dangers and limits. Better to do that in ritual space and with a good commander than at the post office or in a bar.

I have seen so much passive-aggressiveness and aimless anger in my work with social activists that I know nonviolence does not come easily or naturally to people. Even peace work can be a cover for the dark warrior. Often the violence has only gone underground. I have met men in the military who are more in charge of their aggressiveness, in the best sense of that word, than many church folks and peaceniks. In short, if you do not initiate the warrior part of a man, the dark warrior will always win, even by default or denial. As in all exorcisms, someone must say to the possessed, "Show yourself!" (Isaiah 49:9) or "What is your name?" (Mark 5:10) so we can deal with what is really there.

Some drill sergeant or spiritual masters might even say, "Show your best self!" Maybe we could call that positive exorcism because often our best self is as denied and hidden as our demons. The true spiritual teacher makes it safe for you to show yourself as you are and to show your best self. He knows that your best self will follow from your true self.

THE WISE MAN

But if you wish to know how things come about, desire not understanding: ask for grace not instruction, the groaning of prayer not diligent reading, the Spouse not the teacher, God not man, darkness not clarity, not light but the fire.
—ST. BONAVENTURE, *THE SOUL'S JOURNEY TO GOD*

Martin Buber, Karl Rahner, Thomas Aquinas, C. S. Lewis, and Cardinal Newman did not lose their fascination with the wise man, educated academic, or literary male, but integrated their knowledge and research into global, cosmic, and divine concerns. They became men for others instead of just storehouses of information. The magician is the man who integrates his left-brain knowledge into the bigger and often nonrational realm of wisdom. They are not satisfied with being technicians or mere academics. The uninitiated man stops with the accumulation of facts and information; he does not discipline it (warrior), taste it (lover), or integrate it with the big picture (king).[61] Without these, he becomes a stuffy and arrogant curmudgeon, a narrow specialist, a withdrawn dreamer, an office bureaucrat.

I have seen pettiness, envy, and ambition in university faculties and clergymen that rival the business world. These are not magicians, but men trapped in the same small and calculative mind as everybody else. I think it is fair to say that there needs to be some element of spirituality for a man to be a wise man. It is the only thing strong enough to lead him beyond his limited intellect. This is why all higher disciplines of prayer, meditation, and contemplation give you ways to stop the mind or go beyond the mind. The mind cannot help you to be present, much less experience the larger presence; in fact, the mind gets in the way. Perhaps you have heard the unkind old line, "You can be a bishop (or any other official wise man for that matter) without being either smart or holy." The mind can be a doorway, but it can also be a primary barrier to enlightenment. If we do not *both validate and then challenge* the life of the mind, we cannot create the sage. That process is called contemplation or meditation.

I think the early Franciscans and Dominicans made a very strong attempt to initiate the intellectual.[62] They emphasized contemplation, obedience, and poverty as ways to keep the thinker out of his head and connected to the real world of social relationships and to his primary divine relationship. The friars were sent off to Oxford, Paris, Cologne, or Bologna, where they held and established theology chairs, but they were first and last humble friars who lived a life of prayer and service, prior to their academic career. Francis told us that we could do any work or study "as long as it did not extinguish the spirit of prayer and devotion," which always had to come first.

In a very short time, this balancing act produced saintly scholars like St. Bonaventure, Blessed John Duns Scotus, Roger Bacon, St. Thomas Aquinas, Meister Eckhart, St. Albert the Great, Blessed Raymond Lull, and St. Anthony of Padua. And that is only the very short list. You *can* be brilliant and faith-filled at the same time. In general, what you see in the true sage is a balancing act between knowing and not knowing, between intelligence and not needing to be intelligent, between darkness and light. As the book of Proverbs puts it, "To conceal knowledge is the glory of God, to sift it thoroughly is the illusion of kings" (25:2). The wise man also knows that he does *not* know. This humble window of openness, *this willingness to know that we do not know,* has a much used and misused word to describe it: faith. Jesus praises it even more than love.

Perhaps you can hear some of this wisdom from a magus even today. Victor Frankl, the Jewish psychologist who influenced so many people in our lifetime, said it freshly and scarily: "Sell your cleverness and purchase bewilderment instead!" It is such willingness to live with bewilderment that characterizes the true wise man.

THE LOVER

Even after all this time, the sun never says to the earth, "You owe me." Look what happens with a love like that; it lights up the whole sky.   — HAFIZ, SUFI MASTER AND POET

Do you think St. Francis really stopped being the king of the parties? Do you think David of the dance, the psalms, the harp, and many women ever stopped being erotic? Could Rumi, Kabir, Tagore, or Hafiz have possibly written their sacred poetry if they were not sensuous and sensual men? Did St. Philip Neri really stop telling jokes and drinking wine? Did Mozart ever stop having fun? Did the cloistered contemplatives not know joy? I don't think so. They just moved joy and pleasure to the highest level, which is the very definition of a mystic. The contemplative, or saint, is the most refined and highest level of the lover archetype.[63]

It is strange that the West has largely created cultures of conspicuous consumerism, when it took as its ultimate hero and God figure a poor and simple man. You would think our God figure would be Dionysius or Pan. Why do most Eastern and Native peoples of the world consider the West to be greedy and materialistic? Why do we produce such a high rate of physically addicted people? Why is the search for affluence and pleasure our main concern? Could it be because we have not blessed the good side of joy and pleasure? Now it comes back and bites us from behind. *When I consciously seek a certain amount of creature comfort in my life, I find that it satisfies me, and also will never satisfy me.* That is a very life-giving and creative tension to live in.

I do not find the same kind of approach and avoidance attitudes toward pleasure in Hindu countries, among most Jews, and surely not among Native peoples. The lover part of a man was never paid his dues or given legitimate permission in Western Christianity. As many say, sexuality and sensuality is our ever recurring and "unhealed wound."[64] Like petulant schoolboys, we Christians sneak all the fun that we can at the expense of underdeveloped countries, our neighbors, and the health of our own bodies and souls. We feel duly guilty about it all, but we don't usually stop. We priests deny ourselves sex, but then we insist on four-star hotels and restaurants. Carnival in Catholic countries became a necessary decadence to justify receiving the ashes the next morning. Something has not come to balance inside us, and we remain schizoid. We go to the outer world for our daily pleasures, but we seldom allow them to bring us to God, or even to ourselves. We remain split. Flesh is bad and Spirit is good in our terrible dualism. Yet the Christian religion is supposed to be incarnation—a love affair between flesh and spirit. It is really quite strange.[65]

Ours is the only religion in the world that dares to believe that God became flesh. The only religion that chews on the flesh of God has a very sensuous, sexual symbol for the transformation of the lover; we call it the Eucharist. Christianity says that God is Love but does not appear to really enjoy the lover. Despite all the Bach Masses, Baroque churches, incense, vestments, and luxuriant art, we still made our religion into a moralistic matter instead of a mystical joy. Our operative God image was much more a banker, a judge, a timekeeper, or an accountant, but seldom a real lover — in any sense that the normal man understands. Like Michal, the daughter of Saul, we despise David for dancing half naked in church (1 Samuel 6:16); we look away from Shakers, Pentecostals, and holy rollers. Religion should be a proper and dignified thing, we think. The hot sins for the Baptists and Catholics are always associated with the body. This is no religion of incarnation.

Frankly, it is the Hindu sacred poets, Sufi mystics like Rabi'a and Rumi, the Christian saints like John XXIII, Hildegard of Bingen, Francis of Assisi, Julian of Norwich and Therese of Lisieux, or Jewish masters, like the Baal Shem Tov, Abraham Heschel, and Martin Buber, who seem to have met a lover God. The mystics of all religions know this lover God, but they are never allowed to set the tone for the ordinary Christian, Jew, Hindu, or Muslim on the street. We were all lost in law, customs, and holy wars, which largely nullified any chance of a truly love-based ethic for any of the three monotheistic religions. As Paul said so strongly, reliance upon moralisms makes grace impossible (Galatians 3), and it even leads to the death of the soul (Romans 7). Moralisms keep us making lists for God instead of making love to God.[66]

In short, if religion does not integrate and validate the sensual, pleasure-loving, erotic part of a man, it takes devious and destructive directions. If you do not bless it and bow to it, it turns on you and controls you, as we have seen in the recent pedophile scandal. If you bless it, it also shows its limited value and longs for something higher. *The most loving men I have met, the most generous to society and to life, are usually men who also have a lusty sense of life, beauty, pleasure, and sex — but they have very realistic expectations of them.* The smaller pleasures have become a stairway and an invitation to higher ones, almost by revealing simultaneously their wonderful and yet limited character. They offer a first taste but then create a taste for something more and something higher. This is the necessary training of the lover archetype.

The true lover wastes no time in guilt and no time in gluttony either. As Dom Bede Griffiths said, "Sex is far too important to eliminate entirely, and it is far too important to do lightly. The only alternative is to somehow 'consecrate' it." I am personally convinced this is true. The man who took me recently to a four-star restaurant with his elegant wife, while speaking excitedly of the food making love to him, is the same man who talks passionately about refugees, injustice, and Third World issues, and he has passed these passionate concerns on to his children. He is the lover I am talking about.

THE KING/FATHER

When Dad entered the room, the whole world made sense.
— A COUNSELEE

For the king archetype we have grand examples like
Louis IX of France, King Edward of England, Stephen of
Hungary, Thomas More, Pope John XXIII, Martin Luther
King, many U.N. secretaries-general, and Nelson Mandela. These men did not avoid power but owned it,
integrated it, and used it for the common good. Unfortunately we know that they are the exception in history,
and of course, most kings are not heads of state at all.
We created a sacred rite for the consecration of kings
to tell them they must be holy, but we must admit that
it seldom worked. Most of them seem to have handled
power and mercy very poorly, being either dark kings or
warriors.

The king is the integration and recapitulation of the
other three: warrior, magus, and lover. He holds them together in a grand display of balance and wholeness. He
is the master of all power, so much so that he can risk
looking powerless. It took King David a while to become
a king, but he is the symbolic whole man of Judaism, just
as Jesus is the king of kings and whole man for Christians.
Such kingship might be rare, but we must still name it and
present it as the ultimate male goal and the final and full
integration of the sacred.[67] We need good leaders. Yet a
king is not just a leader, he is not just a father, he is our
contact with the holy and with the universal. The kingly
part of a man connects heaven and earth, spiritual and
material, divine and human, inner and outer. When you
meet a man who seems a bit larger than life, you know he
has some king energy. He is a *grand* father.

The dark king is illustrated by Saul, Herod, Pilate, Stalin, and Hitler. They have no vision of the whole, no great realm to hold together, only their small self-interest. The dark king excludes and eliminates the enemy. The true king includes and transforms the enemy, like Nelson Mandela who invites his jailers to his inauguration, or Abraham Lincoln's "malice toward none and charity toward all" after the American Civil War. There may be no way to really initiate a king except to lead him through the other three life initiations. He is always God's work of art.

A young prince needs some models along the way to become a king. If he meets some good passionate lovers, great wise men, and inner-outer warriors, he will be well prepared to hold together the whole human realm. He will be a king, even if it is just a king of his limited area of competence. You can be king of the cobbler shop, believe it or not, and the people will come to your court, not so much to have you fix their shoes as to have you fix their souls. And they will not even know that is why they came.

Classic male initiation tried a most daring, holy, and holistic thing. It blessed the penis and the naked body, honored holiness, the teacher, and the elder, turned military discipline against the self instead of others, and held the whole thing together inside a sacred wholeness, the natural world, the big picture, or what Jesus would call the Kingdom of God. Most cultures initiated just one or another part of a man, which is why we cannot totally idealize them. With a broad brushstroke, I would say that Asia and aboriginal Australia tended to initiate the magician, Africa and most primal cultures idealized the warrior, the Latin and Mediterranean worlds honored the lover, while Europe and North America have always *sought* to develop the king (which is probably why our culture dominates the earth!). But up to now we have largely been at the little prince stage, and we have produced many dark kings. It is now time for a truly global economy of the male soul. Just as Paul's magnificent analogy said, the different parts of the body "need" one another (1 Corinthians 12:12–30) to create together the cosmic "new man" (Ephesians 2:15) who is the hope of the world. It is this man who is so magnificently pictured on our book cover by Fr. John Giuliani. He calls it "the Mystic Christ."

Twelve

ALL TRANSFORMATION TAKES PLACE IN LIMINAL SPACE

Midway in life's journey, I awoke to find my-self alone in a dark wood.
— DANTE ALIGHIERI, *THE DIVINE COMEDY*,
OPENING STANZA

LIMINAL SPACE is a concept refined by Victor Turner in his classic study on initiation and ritual.[68] The Latin word *limen* means "threshold." Liminality is an inner state and sometimes an outer situation where people can begin to think and act in genuinely new ways. It is when we are betwixt and between, have left one room but not yet entered the next room, any hiatus between stages of life, stages of faith, jobs, loves, or relationships. It is that graced time when we are not certain or in control, when something genuinely new can happen. We are empty, receptive, an erased tablet waiting for new words. Nothing fresh or creative will normally happen when we are inside our self-constructed comfort zones, only more of the same. Nothing original emerges from business as usual. It seems we need some antistructure to give direction, depth, and purpose to our regular structure. Otherwise structure, which is needed in the first half of life, tends to become a prison as we grow older.

135

Much of the work of the biblical God and human destiny itself is to get people into liminal space and to keep them there long enough to learn something essential and genuinely new. It is *the ultimate teachable space.* In some sense, it is the only teachable space. So much so that many spiritual giants try to live their entire lives in permanent liminality. They try to live on the margins and on the periphery of the system so they will not get sucked into its illusions and payoffs. They know it is the only position that ensures continued wisdom, ever broader perspective, and even deeper compassion. Some now cleverly call it "the preferential option for the position of the poor." It can take the form of monks, nuns, hermits, Amish withdrawal, and dropouts of various persuasions, but softer forms too, like people who do not watch TV, people who live under the level of a taxable income, people who make prayer a major part of their day, people who deliberately place themselves in risky situations, which is to displace yourself.

For most of us who cannot run off to the wilderness or the hermitage, the older religions offer temporary and partial liminality in things like pilgrimages, silent retreats, periods of fasting, desert solitudes, and sacred times like Lent and Ramadan. Once-a-week church services do not normally come close to creating liminal space. It takes that long for you just to stop wondering whether you turned off the stove and begin to get the kids — or your errant emotions — under control. There has to be something longer, different, and daring, even nonsensical, to break our comfortable sleepwalk and our compulsive trance.

Liminal space will almost always feel counterintuitive, like a waste of time and not logical or rational at all. In fact, it must break your sense of practicality and function and move you into the nonfunctional world for a time. Suffering and disease have that effect. Vacations achieve their purpose only if we enter into some kind of vacuum or genuine detachment from our regular conveyor belt of life. Remember, it is the things that we cannot do anything *about,* the fateful things, and the things we cannot do anything *with,* the useless things, that invariably do something with us. These are the only times when we are not at the steering wheel and someone else can teach us and lead us.

The bubble of usual order has to be broken by a bit of whimsy, holy uselessness, deliberate disruption or displacement, learning to walk in the opposite direction. In liminal space we sometimes need to not-do and not-perform according to our usual successful patterns. We actually need to fail, fast, and deliberately falter to understand the other dimension of life. We need to fast instead of eating, maintain silence instead of talking, experience emptiness instead of fullness, anonymity instead of persona, pennilessness instead of plentifulness. What could break more assuredly our addiction to ourselves? In liminal space we descend and intentionally do not immediately come back out or up; we seek status reversal instead of status, social displacement instead of social belonging.

Seers have always found it necessary to create some kind of liminal space to see clearly, and then reenter the world with freedom and freshness. Francis called his permanent state of liminality "the life of penance,"[69] and that is the essential and true meaning of the term, although the word "penance" has now been corrupted by individualistic and moralistic meanings. Liminality keeps one in an ongoing state of shadow boxing instead of ego confirmation, living intentionally on the edge, struggling with the dark side of things, calling the center and norm into radical question, keeping the heart open inside chosen difficulties. Old monastic life, early Franciscan life, Catholic workers, many sincere missionaries, and Indian sanyassis have had much the same program. Today people go on long backpack trips or various kinds of cold turkey programs—anything to achieve their needed extreme makeover.

In liminal space we choose the chaos of the unconscious over the control of explanations and answers. Thus the language of initiation is the language of darkness not of light, desert not garden, silence not words. People have to be *taught and guided* in how to live in such an uneasy place. In many initiations that I studied, the boys were left to sit in meaningless silence for days—until they actually yearned for direction and guidance, commonly until their circumcision was fully healed. They sat in their pain together, just as women do at times of bereavement. The grief time, the surrendering time, the time of release is a movement that we have little structure for anymore. Even wakes are quick and efficient.

Remember that "Jesus fasted for forty days and forty nights — *after which* he was hungry" (Matthew 3:2). It takes a lot of work to discover your true and real hunger. Without good spiritual direction, however, you will run from the inner chaos and the aimlessness. Without deliberate practice and training over time, you will not know how to face loneliness, yourself, hurts, personality conflicts, and your inner demons and patterns. In religious life, it was called the *novitiate,* which was really one of the few Western attempts to reestablish an initiation process. Mine lasted for a full year in 1961–1962, and it is probably the main practical reason I am here writing this book.

Liminal space is always holy ground — but it takes a while to get those shoes off of Moses (Exodus 3:5) and for Jacob to realize that he had always been there, but didn't know it (Genesis 28:16). Forty days is probably a minimum period to spend in liminal space, which is why it becomes the symbolic number for Israel (Noah in the flood, Moses on the mountain, Jesus in the desert). One of the most effective ways to avoid liminal space is to be quick, efficient, successful, and goal-oriented. Or to be super-religious on the Right or super-correct on the Left. In either place you will only reconfirm all your crutches, addictions, and false securities.

If it is our temperament to seek security, we will run back to the old room that we have already constructed. If it is our temperament to take risks, we will quickly run to a new room of our own making and liking. Hardly anyone wants to stay on the threshold without answers. It feels like Job sitting on his dung heap, picking at his sores. It is "a narrow place that few know how to inhabit" (Matthew 7:13). None of us like to live in the insecurity of waiting without clear direction, meaning, or closure. True biblical faith, therefore, will always be the minority position, in my experience. God has to teach you how to go there, trust the emptiness, and stay there until you are led back out. The truest word for that is "suffering." New things never happen when you are accumulating more self or more ideas and answers; new things happen when you are constricted and limited, and when what you think of as yourself is temporarily or permanently taken away.[70] That is more and more obvious to me, yet for some reason I still want to deny it and hope it isn't true each time.

Initiation rites were a social structure to teach young men what we call beginner's mind or basic teachability, the humility and openness that come from suffering. Some form of beginner's mind is necessary for initiation to happen.[71] You could also say that the creation of a beginner's mind is the result of entering true liminal space. It makes you attentive and awake. So every initiation takes extensive time to create such a context, and then, as I will describe later, it keeps the edges hot so the boy can cook into a proper stew.

THE LIMINOID

The most common substitute for liminal space is "liminoid" space.[72] It superficially looks like liminal space, but it isn't. Nothing new happens here, only a confirmation of the old. I am afraid we are very expert at offering people the liminoid as a counterfeit form of the liminal. We see entertainment serve as worship; religious consumerism replaces any training in fasting, almsgiving, and prayer; loud music and big crowds substitute for depth or breadth; spectacle substitutes for true catharsis. I expect it of the culture, but I find it strange and disappointing in the churches, synagogues, and mosques. The liminoid feels like the real thing, it feels momentarily renewing, but it is just a diversion and actually reaffirms our ego, our persona, and our capacity for denial. It is not a threshold at all, only more of the same.

The liminoid is a movement into trance and unconsciousness so nothing real will be revealed and the shadow has no possibility of showing itself. Victor Turner calls this ceremony, as opposed to true ritual.[73] True ritual, like true drama, always creates a catharsis, or emotional cleansing. It reveals instead of disguises. We love ceremony, the liminoid, because it asks so little of us except to show up, yet it allows us to think we have done something significant. Religion comes to require only attendance, serving as a mere spectator sport. (If you doubt that, come and listen to Catholics sing!) We fear true ritual, at least I do, because it demands psychic and personal participation, and maybe even a change of mind or heart. Basically, the liminoid allows us to remain in our trance.

The systems of this world mostly offer us pseudo initiations, liminoid instead of liminal experiences. They do not open the door to a new universe, to real realignment, just self-talk inside our head. It is like rearranging the deck chairs on the *Titanic;* the real problem or issues are never looked at. Liminoid initiations would be things like smoking, one's first sexual encounter, driving a car, breaking the rules, leaving home, or going alone to Europe. This is necessary first-stage stuff, but it is not transformational in any substantial sense. It defines the self by reaction *against the past* and *choices for* the young man — which are only first-half-of-life issues. Separation from and choice for is the necessary way that the ego creates itself as a self, giving itself boundaries and definition. Initiation is exactly the opposite, a falling into larger union, a surrendering of ego boundaries for the sake of something greater. Initiation is a deep yes to otherness, instead of any superficial self-assertion or self-denial. This is why both Jesus and the Buddha mistrusted acts of mortification, dietary laws, or any religion of heroics. They are usually liminoid, experiences passing for liminal. The Christian liturgical season of Lent is ideally forty days of practice at some form of liminality; Ramadan would

be the same for Moslems, the dreamtime for Aboriginal peoples, the sweat lodge for many Native Americans,
every Sabbath for the Jews, and public worship for all
believers. They are structured liminal space, structured
desire for consciousness, for freedom, and for true presence. As the Jewish tradition brilliantly intuited: if at least
one-seventh of life is not consciousness, presence, and
naked human *being,* the other six days will be caught up
as human *doings* that have little depth, meaning, or final
effect. If at least one-seventh of life is somehow Sabbath
and sabbatical, the rest will take care of itself. Without
daily, weekly, and yearly choices for liminal space, our
whole lives eventually become liminoid and we end up
just doing time.

Thirteen

SO HOW DO WE DO IT?

The eternal truths cannot be transmitted mechanically; in every epoch they must be born anew from the human psyche.
— CARL JUNG, *AFTER THE CATASTROPHE*

ONE WAY OF CREATING liminal space is through what we call ritual or liturgy, through the use of movement, symbol, gesture, art, and story, along with sacred and authoritative words. Good ritual is always somehow about love and death, but in a distilled form and a concise frame. When we "get it" in a confined and compressed space, we can then start seeing the mystery everywhere, and any split between the sacred and profane eventually breaks down. The temple and church are only to get you started; they are not a place to stay. Temple, church, and mosque should teach you *how* to see, but *what you need to see is outside and everywhere*. Many people, especially clergy, just keep shouting, "The sanctuary, the sanctuary, the sanctuary!" The prophet Jeremiah cautions that we should "put no trust in delusive words like these" (Jeremiah 7:4).

Unfortunately, it is largely our work and occupation, television, magazines, and movies, that tell us what to see and how to see. The business world and the media world are the two remaining cultural institutions that form our consciousness (family, church, marriage, school, and the

143

legal system largely being discredited now). Business and media offer the grid that most people are looking through now, even if they are unaware of doing so. You can see why good liturgy and effective ritual is more important than ever—if it leads us into true liminality and back out again. It is the only way out of our sleepwalk, except for suffering and awe, as we said earlier.

Symbols for men have to be graphic, brutal, honest, hard, and almost archetypal or they will not break through the male wall of unconsciousness and denial. It is probably why so many men are fascinated by the images of *Star Wars* and *Lord of the Rings,* any grand displays of good versus evil, or any movies that give them a peek into other exotic and terrifying worlds. If the image does not have some form of risk or violence in it, men are hardly interested. I cannot find a male initiation rite that does not include blood, real physical contact, nakedness, physical endurance, earth or mud connection, a bit of apparent brutality, like cutting and scarring, sweat, saliva, and even semen. Circumcision was not considered the mutilation of the penis but the sacralization of it. Males love this stuff, for some reason, and women don't have a clue why. Just look at male novels, sports, comic books, and horseplay.

It takes a direct hit to get many men's attention. In fact, as one young Austrian man told me, "I would sooner have my dad's direct hits any day than the indirect way that my mom dealt with me. I never knew what the message was from my mom, where it was coming from, what it was for, the intensity of her upset, if there was any message beyond her anger itself, or, worst of all — if there was anything I could do about it. With my dad the message was clear and simple and upfront. He would bop me on the head or punch my shoulder with the same hand that also squeezed me." In this time when our sisters are rightly telling us that they are different than we are, we must have the right to say the same. Men are different than women, and soft sacraments frankly have not worked for many men. Church became a women's thing in most countries, and the men who want to operate in a sanctuary and sacristy notion of religion are few and far between. Around age twelve, boys want to stop dressing up and being altar boys.

My thesis here, common opinion to the contrary, is that most official church rituals appeal much more to the feminine psyche than to the masculine.[74] For all of the patriarchal structure of the church, its symbols and liturgies are very feminine: aesthetically controlled and color-coordinated, lace and silk, incense and candles, doll-like statues that sometimes need changes of clothing, stylized forms that are almost choreography, and just prettiness in general. Since Protestants don't go in for all of that, they make up for it with sentimental art, music, and jargon that does not feed the mind of the ordinary male. For the man on the street and the working man in general, church ritual and sanctuary stuff is foreign terrain instead of sacred space. They are bored to death and want to get away, even when it is done well.

It is no surprise that despite the current political correctness, many people are returning to same-sex high schools. It seems that men, at least, learn better through direct hits, through action and movement, and through ritualized behavior than through lectures, sharing, and words that describe their feelings. I have given conferences all over the world and watched both men and women create appropriate rituals. They are very different (as long as the clergy and official patterns do not control the planning). Women go toward nature symbols, poetry, and all kinds of creative ways to connect personally and to symbolize meanings. They are naturals at it, even if it is often a bit much from the male perspective. Men go toward graphic theater and symbol, often doggerel and literal, even sentimental, but it is sometimes brilliant and heart-stopping. I see the latter in Jesus, who in that sense is very much a man and even more a layman.

A LOVER'S CRITIQUE

The awesome mysteries about which it is forbidden to speak,
this awesome rite of initiation, the spine chilling and holy rites
of initiation.   —ST. JOHN CHRYSOSTOM, *DESCRIPTIONS OF BAPTISM*
IN THE FOURTH CENTURY

I ask your forbearance in the paragraphs ahead. For those of you raised in the church, I might seem too critical. I have no desire to be so because I believe negative energy only creates more negative energy, and it yields no real life or sincere searching. We have no time for that. *Only love can finally be entrusted with the truth;* all other holders will distort truth and even destroy it. My criticisms come as an insider and a lover of the great tradition that John Chrysostom describes above. I hope I have earned some right to say these things since I have given my life to the church as a seeming professional. It is the church that has taught me the values by which I criticize the church. It is love for the message and the messenger that allows me to question the effectiveness of the vehicle for that message. And quite frankly, I want to know what happened to those "spine chilling" liturgies of the fourth century. We need them desperately.

We can contrast most official church rituals (Roman Catholic, Orthodox, Protestant, and Evangelical) with what we saw Jesus doing. All of our traditions have created a set of sanctuary symbols, which are immediately recognizable as such, and therefore sacred. They are churchy and therefore holy: stained-glass windows, organs, icons, crosses, choir robes, sacramental symbols, and decorated pulpits. Jesus presented something very different indeed. He named things holy, or usable by God, before they were made churchy or pulled into the sanctuary. I can hardly think of a single temple or synagogue symbol that he used, unless he changed or transposed its meaning; for example, he named himself the "living water," evoked by the poured water jars (John 7:37–39), the "light of the world" (John 8:12) in comparison to the festal torch on the last day of the Feast of Tabernacles, and the bread of the Passover meal at the Last Supper.

Most of the time we see Jesus operating outside official sacred space, which is very telling. He does most of his work on the streets, in private homes, and in the countryside. He is comfortable with body contact with people in general and women in particular, with dead bodies, with sick bodies, with public and private sinners, with lepers, and with the ritually impure. There are mentions of public bathings and washings down by the riverside, at the Sheep Pool and the pool of Siloam, which were not religious space; he actively used things like saliva and mud paste, which we would surely call New Age or pagan if someone did the same today. He created his own symbol system, although clearly drawing upon the cultural and religious ones that he knew his people would understand. He was a symbolic artist.

But most dangerously of all, Jesus broke the liturgical rules and the deep Jewish sensibilities on a number of occasions. At the official Passover meal, he not only changed the ritual toast of many cups to the *one cup*, which they all drank from, but even worse he asked Jewish boys to drink "blood"! (Check out what Leviticus 17:10–12 has to say on that one!) If there were any homophobic or emotionally withheld types among the twelve, I cannot imagine what they made of John with his head on the breast of Jesus during a proper religious ceremony. He also gave communion to Judas, clearly an unworthy one who was already set to betray him. This is much more on the side of antistructure than structure, more on the side of change that catches one's attention than mere repetition of rubrics. He even legitimated his own disciples' breaking of the sacred Sabbath rule and David eating the sacred bread, and he appealed to an obscure and somewhat mismanaged text to justify it (Luke 6:1–5). It is strange that we would try to make Jesus into a cathedral master of ceremonies. Liturgical protocol does not seem to be his concern in the least. Yet minute rubrics were a major part of my final years of seminary training and have returned with a vengeance from recent Roman instructions.

Jesus's language was not formal or academic language; it was more what we would call the vernacular language or the dialect, using folksy metaphors about regular life, farmers, fishermen, housewives, and daily occurrences. He was more concerned about making sense to the outcasts than to the in-crowd. He downplayed titles and pedigree and status symbols. He mentioned clothing only twice, one time to criticize the priests in their "robes and tassels" and the other to say "that it is only the pagans who worry about such things." He felt free to change customs and seeming commandments.[75] He was not a priest or even a Levite; clearly he was a layman who was not formally trained. Yet after all this, we have created liturgical orders in his honor, with detailed and enforced protocols in both Catholic and Protestant versions, to worship a man *who never once asked to be worshiped, but only followed*. We dress up for a man who tried to dress us down. We create elaborate ceremonies for a man who seldom seemed to have attended any.

I would assert that Jesus was being very much a man and very much a layman in the way he practiced religion. Today's religious male has been told that to be religious he should be feminine, sensitive, churchy, and what some call SNAGs (Soft New Age Guys); and it is not working or even appealing to most of the men of the world. Jesus did not appeal to the in-house and security-seeking types, but to fishermen, businessmen, and zealots. In fact, it was the churchy types who gave him the hardest time. There are statistics that reveal the paltry participation of men in church services in most of the world, and I have seen it myself in country after country. Presently only 28 percent of attendees at Catholic services in the United States are men, and in my experience, they are largely a passive 28 percent at that. Don't believe me; just watch when they come, where they sit, whether they sing, and how quickly they leave.

Now remember, I am not half as hard on Christianity or organized religion as Jesus was on his religion, yet even his strongest tirade in Matthew 23 ends with a final warning against any kind of "refusing" or oppositional attitude toward anything. He cautions us to *be positive, open, and welcoming to reality:* "When you can say, 'Bless-ings on him who comes in the name of the Lord'" (v. 39), you will be ready. So we sing it as the warm-up song, which we call the Sanctus. We have to be prepared and practiced in saying yes because it is always much harder to say than no. Yes is always a surrendering of ego bound-aries, and that answer makes us feel weak and vulnerable afterward. Saying no, which contracts our ego boundaries into a proper self, makes us feel strong, safe, and even su-perior. Be careful when you say no, and pay attention to what space your responses are coming from.

Whatever no we say in life must come out of a previ-ous and fundamental yes. Isaiah, Jeremiah, Amos, and Ezekiel spoke strongly, and sometimes bitterly, against military alliances, militarism, court prophets, temple sac-rifice, self-serving priesthood, ritualism, and salvation by ancestry or group membership; yet one never doubted that it was their encounter with "the Holy One of Israel" that gave them such criticism and such urgency. Their central energy was utterly positive, and you can feel the difference. The biblical prophets had learned to say yes to God and life before they dared to say no to anything, which changed their entire program and goal. It is the unique role of a biblical prophet, somewhat rarely copied, I am afraid.

Jesus's and even Paul's attempts to reform their reli-gion — and that is what they both thought they were doing[76] — were not anti-Semitic any more than I am anti-Catholic. Give them more credit than that. They were *anti all religion when it served itself* instead of serving God or transformation into God. Religion is best when it points beyond itself, like Isaiah and John the Baptist. It is worst when it gives you just enough of the form to inoculate you against the substance, when it substitutes rituals for the reality, the container for the contents, the wineskins for the wine.

Judaism did the same in Leviticus and Numbers, but this only revealed the archetypal pattern that Christianity and Islam would soon repeat down to small detail. Every religion does this in some sense. Buddhist temples in the Orient can be filled with lustful and security-seeking monks and nuns, Hindu fakirs can be fakers, Orthodox monks at Mount Athos can be trapped in petty moralisms and misogyny, and American fundamentalism has raised ignorance and arrogance to an art form. No one group has a monopoly on mediocrity, and yet *every group has a tie to the eternal and usually holds on to one or another precious truth*. If you want precious truth bad enough, you will be patient with all of the religions. They share in the same imperfection that we must forgive in ourselves.

Fourteen

JESUS'S FIVE MESSAGES
The Common Wonderful

*Was there ever a word so majestic, from one
end of heaven to another? Was anything
ever heard like this? Did ever a people hear
the voice of the living God speaking from the
heart of the fire, as you have heard it—and
still remain alive?* —DEUTERONOMY 4:32–33

*For anyone who is linked with all that lives
always has hope.* —ECCLESIASTES 8:4

*Happy the eyes that see what you see, for
I tell you prophets and kings wanted to see
what you see, and never saw it; to hear what
you hear and never heard it.* —LUKE 1:23–24

IF THE FIVE PROMISES of initiation seemed hard or negative to you, I want to also give you the energizing
source that makes them possible and that becomes their
long-term effect. I call this "the common wonderful," the
collective beauty and security that healthy people live
within, no matter what words they use for it. Some have
called the promises "the five positive messages." The common wonderful is a cosmic egg of meaning that will hold
you, help you grow, and give you ongoing new birth and
beginnings. It is your underlying worldview, your matrix
for life, your energy field that keeps you motivated each

day; it answers your basic questions of life. It operates largely subliminally, but very powerfully.

The five messages are not so much *taught* during initiation as radically presumed in some way by the elders and therefore *caught* by the initiates. They were the divine harmony out of which initiation was born and created. This catching is, in fact, *the very heart and center of the initiation experience.* It is this utterly grounding and peace-filling experience that gives the initiate the courage to accept and face the initiation's five ego-stripping messages that we talked about earlier in the book.

The five positive messages must be a young man's own inner experience, not something he believes because others told him to; they must be something he *knows to be true for himself.* The five negative messages must be deliberately taught and ritualized because we all will resist their truth, run from them, and even deny them if we can. I present this cosmic egg of meaning, the common wonderful, only on the final morning of a Men's Rite of Passage, and most men by then know it to be true. In fact, they are swimming in it! Yet I have never preached any of this directly. Thus begins a positive and ever-deepening search for the initiated man. (I will use New Testament quotes that most of us will be familiar with here, although there are similar messages in all the great traditions, especially from the Islamic mystics, the Hasidic Jews, and the Hindu holy men.)

1. IT IS TRUE THAT LIFE IS HARD, BUT:

"My yoke is easy and my burden is light."

(MATTHEW 11:28)

It is hard to hear God—but it is even harder *not* to hear God. The pain one brings upon oneself by living outside of evident reality is a greater and longer-lasting pain than the brief pain of facing it head on. Enlightened people invariably describe the spiritual experience of God as resting, peace, delight, and even ecstasy. Often the saints and mystics used even more erotic and sensuous metaphors. John of the Cross speaks of being seized by the same delight that is in God, being caught into God's great being, and breathing God's same air. St. Bernard said that for him, Jesus was "honey in the mouth, music to the ear, and joy in the heart." Hafiz, Rumi, Tagore, and Kabir made life with God sound downright fun and fantastic, a poem instead of a trial.

If your religion has no deep joy, has no inherent contentment about it, then it is not the real thing. If your religion is primarily fear of self, the world, and God, if it is primarily a need to tend to religious duties and obligations, then it is indeed a hard yoke and heavy burden and hardly worthwhile. One wonders why so many people bother with such chosen unhappiness.[77] I think the promise from Jesus that the burden is easy and light seeks to reassure us that rigid and humorless religion is not his way, or even the way. St. Francis de Sales said that you would "catch many more flies with a teaspoon of honey than with a gallon of vinegar." Surely God knows that too.

Seek joy in God and peace within yourself; seek to rest in the good, the true, and the beautiful. It is God within you who loves God. It will be the only resting place that will allow you to also hear and bear the darkness. Hard and soft, difficult and easy, pain and ecstasy do not eliminate one another, but actually allow each other. They bow back and forth like dancers, although it is harder to bow to pain and to failure. *If you look deeply inside every success, there are also seeds and signs of failure; if you look inside every failure, there are also seeds and signs of success.* To see that is foundational to wisdom, and it is an axiom of basic spiritual seeing.

You can bear the hardness of life and see through failure if your soul is resting in a wonderful and comforting sweetness and softness. That's why people in love — and often people at the end of life — have such an excess of energy for others. If your truth does not set you free, it is not the truth at all. If God cannot be rested in, he must not be much of a God. If God is not juice and joy, then what has created all these lilacs and lilies?

2. IT IS TRUE THAT YOU ARE NOT THAT IMPORTANT, BUT:

"Do you not know that your name is written in heaven?"

(LUKE 10:20)

If we know our original blessing, we can easily handle our original sin. If we rest in a previous dignity, we can bear insults effortlessly. If you really know your name is on some eternal list, you can let go of the irritations on the small lists of time. Ultimate security allows you to suffer small insecurities without tremendous effort. If you are tethered at some center point, it is amazing how far out you can fly and not get lost. We need a still point in this twirling world of images and feelings. If you know you are a beloved son of the Father, other fathers and mothers cannot finally hurt you.

If there is no list of names in eternity, we are burdened with making our own personal name day after day. Either we are made by another or we must be self-made. Then it is every man for himself, dog eat dog, as we vie with one another for a zero-sum dignity and importance. If you have it, then I don't, or I will use you for my measuring stick. In either case, I am lost in comparison, envy, competition, and codependency. *Spiritually: if you have it, I do too, and if I have it, you do too.* Authentic spirituality is an experience of abundance and mutual flourishing instead of scarcity. Material gifts and ego gifts decrease with usage, whereas spiritual gifts actually increase with each use, in ourselves and in those around us.

If you have no foundational significance, you must constantly attempt to self-signify and self-validate. Everyone is then a competitor and rival. You cannot help but be pushed around by your neediness and your judgments, and you will push others around too. I don't know which is worse. If you have no unshakable experience, you will be lost in fragile momentary experiences that cannot be sustained or really enjoyed. What we are facing is a huge crisis of meaning today, which leads to every form of addiction to fill that aching hole. *The soul needs meaning as much as the body needs food.* The effect is an addictive society that constantly ups the ante of need and desire because the last ones have never satisfied.[78] It creates the very shape of consumer cultures like our own.

Our world today is described by the Greek myth of Sisyphus, the king of Corinth, who was tortured by having to roll a rock to the top of the hill, only to have it always roll back down again. Futility and meaninglessness are directly correlated to addiction, in my opinion. When we have meaning, we need very little else. When we don't have meaning, we can never have enough toys. Somehow we must find that foundational meaning for our lives, or we will try to pull ourselves up by our own bootstraps. It can't be done, and you are miserable while you are trying. You must find your North Star outside your own little comparative system or you will be lost in rivalry

and daily defeat. It is a whole different way of looking
at what we mean by God saving us. God first of all saves
us from ourselves, our emotional neediness and hurt, and
our obsessive-compulsive mind games. Then *the truth of
being* is obvious and all around us.

Your importance is given and bestowed in this universe, which is the unbreakable covenant between you
and your Creator. You are declared important; you cannot declare yourself important. To attempt it is delusional
behavior. When a Zen master tells you about the face
you had before you were born, when Jesus tells you that
"your name is written in heaven," when Isaiah tells you
that "God has branded you on the palms of his hands"
(49:16), they have saved you tens of thousands of dollars
in self-promotion fees, tap dance lessons, and therapy for
your negative self-image. The problem we try so hard to
solve is already completely solved, and most people don't
know it.

3. IT IS TRUE THAT YOUR LIFE IS NOT ABOUT YOU, BUT:

*"I live now not my own life, but the life of Christ who lives
in me."* (GALATIANS 2:20)

*"Your life is hidden with Christ in God. He is your life, and
when he is revealed, you will be revealed in all your glory
with him."* (COLOSSIANS 3:4)

All the truly great persons I have ever met are characterized by what I would call "radical humility." They
are deeply convinced that they are drawing from another
source; they are an instrument. Their genius is not their
own; it is borrowed. So they end up doing great and ex-
pansive things precisely because they do not take first
or final responsibility for their gift; they don't worry too

much about their failures, nor do they need to promote themselves. Their life is not their own, yet at some level they know that it has been given to them as a sacred trust. Someone has taken them seriously. They feel deeply respected, which I always say is all that men really want.

It is like someone has quietly deposited a million dollars in your checking account, and now it is secretly yours, yet you always know it was a gift. It is yours to use and enjoy and expand, but you cannot say you earned it or you deserved it. Everybody thinks it is your money and admires you for it, but you know better and cannot take the credit. You just live in gratitude and confidence, and you try to let the flow continue through you. You know that love can be repaid by love alone.

Great people do not need to concoct an identity for themselves; they merely try to discover, uncover, and enjoy the identity they already have. As Francis said to us right before he died in 1226, "I have done what was mine to do. Now you must do what is yours to do." Yet to just be yourself, who you really are, warts and all, feels like too little, a disappointment, a step backward into ordinariness. Most Christians write it off as a cheap humanistic cliché. It sounds much more exciting to pretend I am St. Francis than accepting that I am Richard and that that is all God expects me to be — and everything that God expects me to be. My destiny and his desire are already written in my genes, my upbringing, and my natural gifts. It is probably the most courageous thing you will ever do to accept that you are just yourself. It will take perfect faith, the blind yes of Mary, because it is the ongoing and same incarnation. Just like the word of God descending into one little whimpering child, in one small stable, in one moment, in one unimportant country, noticed by no-body. We call it *the scandal of particularity.* This, here, now, me always feels too small and specific to be a dwelling place for God! How could I be taken this seriously?

This is the nature of the fall that is Adam's primal suffering, so do not think this is something new. Adam fell into separateness and self-loathing. As Henri Nouwen once shared with me personally, he believed that original sin could only be described as "humanity's endless capacity for self-rejection." Adam thought he had left the garden, and he had, but the garden fortunately never left him. In the very first conversation that God had with humanity, Yahweh questions Adam about his self-doubt and the self-loathing that came from his feeling cut off. "Who told you that you were naked?" he asks Adam (Genesis 3:11), almost as if to say, "I sure didn't!" Immediately Yahweh, in a most nurturing and protective image, "made clothes and put them on him" (Genesis 3:21). God is always covering our nakedness and silencing our shame. Only the original manufacturer can declare what the product—you—should be. Nobody else. Your identity is written in your genes and enjoyed by God precisely in its specificity. God only creates individually, and not genus and species. "Why, every hair of your head has been counted," as Jesus puts it (Matthew 10:30). God chooses us into existence, and decides for us every minute, or we would fall into non-being. We are forever included, and Jesus's metaphor for that realization is a wedding banquet to which nobody wants to come! God, poor God, has a very hard time giving away God.

So we cannot really find ourselves at all; the great ones consistently speak of *being found,* like a prodigal son. "I once was lost, but now I'm found, was blind but now I see" is the perennial experience. Western philosophy surely reached its low point in Descartes' infamous "I think, therefore I am." We now know that the truth is exactly the opposite: "I think, therefore I am not." My thinking is *not* me; it is the primary substitute for me and the place to hide from moving from pure and simple presence to being. Most people stay in their ideas and avoid that humiliating collapse back into naked being, or as we believers would say, "Falling into the hands of the living God is a fearful thing" (Hebrews 10:31). Remember always that God and being are the same thing. *Deus est Ens,* St. Thomas Aquinas said. The simplicity of it is a blow to our intelligence and an utter surrendering of our will-to-power. The challenge is to risk being both one and many, united to all, and yet me. In Christian theology this is revealed in the mystery of a trinitarian God, who is also both one and many.[79] Even "God the Father's life is not about him," but it is about the Son and the Spirit. It is that core love dynamism that makes the whole universe a constant flow.

In the spiritual life, what we think we are doing is actually being done to us. All we can do is say yes to it. "When he is revealed" (the big life), "you will be revealed in all your glory with him," Paul says. You will find yourself inside the other and held by the other, your own glory intact and protected. This true self is ironically much more glorious, grounded, original, and free than any self-manufactured persona could ever be. We are interrelated with being, participating in the very life of God, while living out one little part of that life in our own exquisite form.

Paradoxically, I will end this section by saying with new freedom the exact opposite. *Your life is precisely about you, but now you know who you really are,* and you can hold this fire without burning up and burning out. The Jesuit poet Gerard Manley Hopkins, who was relying upon John Duns Scotus's doctrine of "thisness," says it wonderfully: God creates and chooses each thing individually. This is one of my favorite poems of all time, and it is usually called "As Kingfishers Catch Fire":

> Each mortal thing does one thing and the same;
> Deals out that being indoors each one dwells;
> Selves—goes itself; myself it speaks and spells,
> Crying *What I do is me: for that I came…*
> Acts in God's eye what in God's eye he is—
> Christ—for Christ plays in ten thousand places,
> Lovely in limbs, and lovely in eyes not his,
> To the Father through the features of men's faces.[80]

4. IT IS TRUE THAT YOU ARE NOT IN CONTROL, BUT:

> *"Can any of you, for all your worrying, add a single moment to your span of life?"* (LUKE 12:26)

We are destined to become control freaks in a secular society because there is no one who we know, trust, or like enough to finally hand over control to. In fact, you would be absolutely irresponsible if you did not micromanage everything and engineer every situation. Who else will take care of things, if not you? Is that not the growing and pervasive mentality in every aspect of our lives? Americans and Europeans are, by definition, high-maintenance people. They have grown used to needing a great deal, and needing much control of that great deal. I do not see social relations, marriage, politics, or job satisfaction getting much easier in the near future, despite all the advances of social psychology, management seminars, and personal therapy. When so many people have been given such a sense of entitlement and deservedness, when taking control of your life has been made into a national mantra, quite contrary to the whole spiritual tradition, we are setting ourselves up for hurt and for hurting one another more than ever before. Not just because of wars and violence, but because our daily lives will just stop being much fun.

If we cannot control the biggies, life and death, why should we spend so much time trying to control all the lesser outcomes? Call it destiny, providence, guidance, synchronicity, or coincidence, if you will, but people who are connected to their source do not need to steer their own life and agenda. They know that it is being done for them in a much better way than they ever could. This is not provable to the logical mind, nor does it mean that you should roll over and play dead. It is a very subtle and discreet art form taught by the Spirit. Those who hand themselves over are received, and the flow happens through them. Those who don't relinquish control are still received, but they significantly slow down the natural flow of Spirit. Again, it all comes back to the basic template of reality that we Christians call Trinity. It is so traditional that it sounds revolutionary, which seems to be the nature of great mystery.

When you set yourself up to think you deserve, expect, or need something to happen, you are setting yourself up for constant unhappiness and a final inability to enjoy or at least allow what is going to happen anyway. After a while, you find yourself resisting almost everything at some level. It is a terrible way to live. After a while, you live your life with one foot on the brake, and you wonder why your accelerator does not work very well. My experience has been that people who burn out are more often than not just halfhearted about what they are doing. Seldom are they really that overworked. Ironically, when you give up your control mechanisms, you are able to live with both feet gently on the accelerator and move with the divine flow. Without all the inner voices of resistance, it is amazing how much you can get done and not get tired. Giving up control is a school of union, compassion, and understanding. It is a school for the final letting go that we call death. Practice giving up control early in life. You will be much happier and much closer to the truth, to the moment, and to God—none of which can be experienced by taking control of your life.

Surrendering to the divine flow is not about giving up, giving in, capitulating, becoming a puppet, being naïve, being irresponsible, or stopping all planning and thinking. Surrender is about a peaceful inner opening that keeps the conduit of living water flowing. It is a quiet willingness to be used as a conduit which allows divinity to transpire. Surrender is a willingness to trust that you really are a beloved son, which allows God to be your Father. It really is that simple.

5. IT IS TRUE THAT YOU ARE GOING TO DIE, BUT:

> *"I am certain of this, neither death nor life, nothing that exists, nothing still to come, not any power, not any height nor depth, nor any created thing can ever come between us and the love of God."* (ROMANS 8:38–39)

It seems that we are born with a longing, desire, and deep hope that this thing called life could somehow last forever. It is a premonition from something eternal that is already within us. Some would call it the soul. Believers would call it the indwelling presence of God. It is God in us that makes us desire God. It is an eternal life already within us that makes us imagine such an impossible thing as eternal life. It is the Spirit of God that allows us to seriously hope for what we only intuit. Thus Paul loves to call the Spirit the first fruits, the promise, the pledge, the guarantee, or the first installment. These are all marvelous metaphors for this instinct for God and for more life that is already planted within us. You cannot imagine something or hope for something if you have not already touched upon it in some small way. All spiritual cognition is actually recognition, as I have said before.

Age upon age, the ancients, the Egyptians, the Native peoples, and most major religions dreamed of immortality and tried to prepare for it and assure it. They mummified, they left food and traveling maps, they saw their ancestors in the stars, in the wind, and in animals, they prayed to the dead and for the dead, and they could not and did not believe that the dead were gone. The ancestors became ghosts, spirits, advocates, and angels, and they went to Hades, Sheol, Heaven, or Nirvana. People knew, hoped, believed, and trusted that an even deeper communion was possible with loved ones after death, and often it seems to be true. Catholics created purgatory so they could still have possibility and some control even after death. It all comes from the immortality instinct. We can't and won't let go of this wonderful thing called life.

And not just life, but eternal love too. If God is so patient and merciful and forgiving and accepting with us day after day in this world, which most religions teach, then why not believe the same is true after death? Why would God change God's tactics or attitude about us when we die? Really! Isn't God one? Isn't God consistent? Is our little human love somehow better than God's? I wouldn't betray or turn on someone that way, I hope; yet we are foolish enough to believe that God would. The gratuitous nature of life finally becomes the gratuitous nature of love too! Just as life is unearned, so is God's love because God's very nature is to love.

Yes, we are going to die, but we have already been given a kind of inner guarantee and promise right now that death is not final—and it takes the form of love. We have our first insurance installment already in hand. Deep in the heart and psyche, love, both human and divine, connotes something eternal and gratuitous, and it does so in a deeply mysterious but compelling way. It cannot be proven; it can only be known by the same quality in you.[81] Love knows love; it completes the circuit. Only love in us can see love over there, which is why God commands us to love. It is not a test or a trial; it is just that until you love yourself, you will not be able to see or allow or enjoy love over there. I call it the principle of likeness. Like recognizes like.

It is the simple experience of love, in the ordinary ways that humans experience love, that imprints on our soul something like this: if love always feels so limitless and unearned and nonrational, then reality itself must be limitless, unearned, and a bit irrational too! That is the heart of all human hope. We cannot make God love us more, and we cannot make God love us less. We do not have that kind of power because God simply is love, and God's love is not determined or changed by its object. It comes from the inner nature of God, who is love (1 John 4:16). What follows, of course, is that if we are God's creature, then maybe love is what we are too. Love is not something we do or ever do perfectly, but love is some-thing we are, something we rest in, and something we learn to draw upon and live in, through, and with.

As Catherine of Siena said so perfectly: "It is heaven all the way to heaven." If you have it now, you will have it then. Love itself, the patterns and persistence of it, the ubiquity and irrationality of it, the wonder and mystery of it, is the code and key to understanding everything else. Absolutely everything. Most simply when we live in love, we will not be afraid to die. We have built a bridge between worlds.

For the garden is the only place there is, but you will
    not find it
Until you have looked for it everywhere and found
    nowhere that is not a desert.
The miracle is the only thing that happens, but to
    you it will not be apparent
Until all events have been studied and nothing
    happens to you that you cannot explain.
Life is the destiny you are bound to refuse until you
    have consented to die.

—W. H. AUDEN, "FOR THE TIME BEING"

Appendix

A SAMPLE RITE

(Envisioning a workable and Western five-day Initiation Rite for adult men; five days is an absolute time minimum.)

CREATING THE SPACE AND ATTITUDE

Keeping the edges hot is a crucial requirement in conducting initiation rites.[82] Basically, it means that the ritual space is defined and protected, often by boundary markers and rules that might seem arbitrary and even nonsensical. Long periods of silence, required clothing, punctuality, rustic accommodations, food, uniformity and even conformity, not calling home, being cut off from outside stimulation, going to bed on time, a certain strictness, and no nonsense are all quite necessary. They create respect for the group and absolute respect for the process. If the edges are cold and the group members are all living inside their own self-centered and distracted pace and space, men will not take the whole process seriously. They will know that you are not that serious about it yourself, and therefore it cannot be that important. Men respect very hot edges and feel respected inside them. Hot edges are a must for creating any kind of liminal or sacred space. Liberal humanistic society has little knowledge or appreciation for this. If you do not have your own thinking clear here, you will not succeed in contemporary

Western society, which is very biased against boundaries, community, requirements, and anything that appears irrational. There can never be mere observers, journalists, or spectators inside liminal space; that would destroy the space's hot edges.

Jews, Catholics, Orthodox, and Moslems still understand hot edges to a much greater degree than most Protestants because they draw from times before the Enlightenment with a much longer understanding of ritual and liminal space. Silence, genuflection, a skull cap and prayer shawl, sign of the cross, prayer beads, bows and prostrations, blessings of space and time, holy water, liturgical seasons, feast days, processions, kneeling and standing as one, fast days, and non-work days have all given these groups some respect for sacred space and kinesthetic knowing. Protestants need to be taught, but they also tend to love sacred space once they understand what they have been missing by limiting religion to the head and words.

I. Separation From

(Application process, preparation, travel to, and opening tone-setting day or half-day)

Moving to a natural world and a safe place.

Creating liminal space, as defined in chapter 12.

Calling forth desire and anticipation.

Slowing down the body and the psyche.

Calling forth the contemplative mind and lessening one's confidence in the calculative mind.

Separating from usual comforts, diversions, roles, security blankets, the media, phones, family, partners, and women. Heating up the edges by eliminating the usual distractions and codependencies.

II. Day of Death

Dramatic symbolization and verbal presentation of the necessary death that precedes all entrance into the true self. Distinguishing the small self and great self.

Much time for silence, slowing down, non-answers, sitting in the spaciousness with anxiety and doubt, creating a longing for guidance and direction.

A stark day to shock the psyche out of its trance and the body out of its complacency.

III. Day of Grief

Descent language and ritual continues, leading men to the world of grief and loss, sadness and surrender. "What have you already lost and not let go of?" "What must you let go of to continue on the journey?" Don't push any of it, just name it and leave open space for the Spirit to lead.

Continued silence, slowing down, and time for developing the contemplative mind and one's *felt* reality.

IV. Day of Initiation

Men are individually blessed and sent into a solitude day in nature with an expectation of meeting God/themselves/ the big picture/their true self. A day of fasting and silence. Formal rituals of initiation that symbolize all of the above end the day, and the five essential messages are communicated at the heart of the day. Night celebration, preferably in nature and around a fire.

V. Day of Reincorporation or Communion

Five positive messages are now also communicated, and a final liturgy (work of the people), communion service, celebration is enjoyed. There are many ways to do the last day. The edges do not need to be so hot or defined. They will be that way naturally, but the elders still lead, though now more as brothers.

Most initiations that I have studied seem to have this overall pattern, although there are many variations, of course. You will have to fill in with your own symbols, stories, and rituals to achieve these primary movements, remembering that the emphasis is on *ritual process* and not just lectures. The communal events must be done with clear and defined hot edges as described in the chapters on ritual, and home groups must meet at least once a day, where each man can share and feel supported in a confidential and deep way, through guided questions that follow the lecture. Remember, however, that this is not a psychological exercise or a therapeutic agenda, but a cosmological realignment. Don't let men preach to one another to avoid self-disclosure about what is happening inside them. "So much holiness is lost to the church because men refuse to share the secrets of their hearts with one another," said John Henry Newman.

BEFORE AND AFTER

For authentic sacred space or truly transformative space, we need:

1. The existence of a community that the initiate can
   be sent from and return to. The community must
   have the wisdom to know how to guide the initiate through the transformation and then confirm it
   afterward by some form of social agreement.

2. Liminal space must be created where the initiate
   can be taken, usually in nature and apart. (Christians created awesome church buildings, music, and
   art; Jews and Native religions more often created
   inner space through sacred stories; Moslems created
   a structured day of ritual prayer.) An alternative universe must be presented and made more real and
   more attractive than this one, so this world can be
   both detached from and then attached to properly.
   Never forget the burning bush, Elijah's cave, Jacob's
   ladder, Mary's annunciation and childbirth, Jesus's
   and John's desert sojourns, or Paul's conversion. They
   all happened outside official sacred space and in the
   natural or workaday world.

3. The male must be separated from business as usual,
   particularly from the feminine, the warm nest, exist-
   ing roles and securities. This is attempted on extended
   solitary retreats and in monastic life by Catholics and
   Orthodox; Jews tend to do it ritually with the concept
   of the male quorum of ten, and the historic bar mitz-
   vah, which was a male gathering. Moslems do it every
   day in the mosque, reflecting the other extreme from
   Catholics. We have passed on religion largely through
   mothers; they pass it on through fathers.

4. Some kind of symbolic death must be experienced.
   The initiate must be led to the edge of his normal resources, so he is forced to rupture planes and gain

access to his true self. Normally this takes the form of solitude, silence, and suffering over an extended time, which are the only things strong enough to break our ego attachment to the false self and move us to a new plane. The language of dying and death is used at Eucharist, and the language of passing over at the Seder, but for Christians it is all idolized in Jesus and projected onto Jesus instead of participated in ourselves. Jews and Christians both overdo the remembrance thing, in my opinion, instead of doing it *again now*. Memorial meals have become just that—memorials.

5. A new birth, a new life, a new status, and a new community are dramatically named and symbolized and celebrated often in effusive ways. "This is your real life," we want to say! The joyous language and symbols of resurrected life are used at Eucharist and Easter but again largely projected onto Jesus and admired there, instead of being uncovered and sought in ourselves, which is the very thing Jesus did and wanted us to do (see John 10:34–36). Some Protestants and Mediterranean Catholics are much better at fellowship and resurrected life theology, and Jews know how to dance, drink, and sing together. Secular Westerners will find spiritual joy a whole new experience, independent of drink, food, money, or success.

6. A change of status that is definitive and closed and achieved, as the church said, *ex opere operato* by the very fact of having done it. You are supposed to be almost metaphysically different after participating in true initiation,[83] just as occurs in several of the

sacraments. There is a clear before and after, not just in form and externals but hopefully in the substantial self. (Some elements of this remain in Catholics' participation at Eucharist, which is perhaps why they still confess *not* doing it. They intuitively know it is fundamentally significant and transformative if the Presence is encountered.[84])

7. One's new spiritual status is recognized and honored by the community, which confirms this interior change in the initiate and effects a socially different person with inherent dignity, which is no longer dependent on achievement or performance. One could even call it justification by faith or validation from outside by sheer gift. This changes the entire psychic framework, and it is part of the magic of initiation, which we no longer enjoy — with disastrous psychological effects for all of us. We seek initiation through various performance principles, trials, and daring feats of skill, instead of asking, waiting, and expecting to be "lifted up by our hair and placed elsewhere," like the prophet Habakkuk (Daniel 14:33ff.).

8. The final coup de grâce is pretty much lost in this age of entitlement and religious formula. The transformative secret of initiation is that it is something very precious that is *given,* not *earned.* There is no way that the small self can make it happen by willpower or technique. The first centuries of the church still knew how to create and sequence spiritual desire, longing, and search. This was held on to for a long time with the Mass of the Catechumens, and people had to leave at a certain point because they were not ready to receive the full gift yet. Now Eucharist

has to do with achieving moral worthiness and passing ritual requirements instead of stirring holy desire. This unfortunately leaves most church rituals outside the realm of radical grace except for those who have done their inner journey and personally experienced it elsewhere.

More Resources for Creating Rites

Campbell, Joseph. *The Hero's Journey.* San Francisco: Harper & Row, 1990.

Downey, Michael. *Digging Deep.* Winona, Minn.: St. Mary's Press, 2003.

Gabriele, Edward Francis. *From Many, One: Praying Our Rich and Diverse Cultural Heritage.* Notre Dame, Ind.: Ave Maria Press, 1995.

Linn, Denise. *Quest: A Guide for Creating Your Own Vision Quest.* New York: Ballantine, 1997.

Mahdi, Louise Carus, Nancy Christopher, and Michael Meade, eds. *Crossroads: The Quest for Contemporary Rites of Passage.* La Salle, Ill.: Open Court, 1996.

Mahdi, Louise Carus, Steven Foster, and Meredith Little, eds. *Betwixt and Between: Patterns of Masculine and Feminine Initiation.* La Salle, Ill.: Open Court, 1987.

Paladin, Lynda. *Ceremonies for Change.* Walpole, N.H.: Stillpoint, 1991.

Rohr, Richard. "Boys to Men: Rediscovering Rites of Passage for Our Time." *Sojourners* (May–June 1998).

Thompson, Keith. *To Be a Man: In Search of the Deep Masculine.* Los Angeles: Tarcher, 1991.

Weiner, Bernard. *Boy into Man: A Father's Guide to Initiation of Teenage Sons.* San Francisco: Transformation Press, 1992.

NOTES

A Word from Richard

1. Please take time to read the titles and authors in the extended bibliography too. It can be an education just to observe the overlapping disciplines and areas of thought that are involved in the issue of male initiation.

2. Richard Rohr, *Quest for the Grail* (New York: Crossroad, 1994). This is the only one of my books ever to win an award, and I think that is because it illustrates the most successful attempt for ordinary Western laymen to describe their spiritual journey in laymen's terms, which they did from around 1180 to 1360 CE.

3. Mircea Eliade, *Rites and Symbols of Initiation* (New York: Harper Torchbooks, 1958); Arnold Van Gennep, *The Rites of Passage* (Chicago: University of Chicago, 1960); Victor Turner, *The Ritual Process* (Ithaca, N.Y.: Cornell University, 1969); Joseph Campbell, *The Hero's Journey* (San Francisco: Harper & Row, 1990); Gilbert H. Herdt, ed., *Rituals of Manhood: Male Initiation in Papua New Guinea* (Berkeley: University of California Press, 1982); Robert Moore, *The Archetype of Initiation* (Philadelphia: Xlibris, 2001).

4. Alan Watts, *The Wisdom of Insecurity* (New York: Vintage, 1951).

5. I cannot find the exact reference, but I know Albert Einstein said it.

6. Richard Rohr, *Everything Belongs,* new edition (New York: Crossroad, 2003).

7. Mary Beth Ingram, C.S.J., *Scotus for Dunces: An Introduction to the Subtle Doctor* (St. Bonaventure, N.Y.: Franciscan Institute Publications, 2003). Most other source books on John Duns Scotus are too technical, too inaccessible, or too expensive. This book is excellent at bringing him down to earth and seeing the implications of his very subtle thought.

8. Richard Rohr, O.F.M., *The NEW Great Themes of Scripture* (Cincinnati: St. Anthony Messenger Press, 1999), ten tapes, #A7090.

9. Elizabeth Johnson, *She Who Is: The Mystery of God in Feminist Theological Discourse* (New York: Crossroad, 1993), and Elisabeth Schüssler Fiorenza, *In Memory of Her* (New York: Crossroad, 1984). These two fine theologians give feminism a very good name and give God a new chance.

10. James Nelson and Sandra Longfellow, eds., *Sexuality and the Sacred* (Louisville: Westminster John Knox, 1994). A mother lode of excellent articles. Also Carter Heyward's excellent *Touching Our Strength: The Erotic as Power and the Love of God* (San Francisco: HarperSanFrancisco, 1989).

11. Richard Rohr, *The Shape of God: What Difference Does Trinity Make?* (Albuquerque, N.Mex.: Center for Action and Contemplation, 2004), a taped conference on God as centripetal force that finally includes all of creation.

Chapter 1: Initiated into What?

12. Karl Jaspers, *The Origin and Goal of History* (Zurich: Artemis, 1949), 19ff.

13. For a classic book that makes this point exquisitely, read Alan Watts, *Behold the Spirit: A Study in the Necessity of Mystical Religion* (New York: Random House, 1947).

14. Ernest Becker, *The Denial of Death* (New York: Free Press, 1973), 11 and passim.

15. Paula D'Arcy and Richard Rohr, *The Spirituality of the Two Halves of Life* (Cincinnati: St. Anthony Messenger Press, 2004), taped retreat.

16. Richard Rohr, *Dying, We Need It for Life* (Cincinnati: St. Anthony Messenger Press, 2002), taped address to Los Angeles Religious Education Congress, #A8271.

Chapter 2: Why We Need Initiation in Modern Cultures

17. Alexander Mitscherlich, *Society without the Father* (New York: Harper Perennial, 1963).

18. Weldon Hardenbrook, *Missing from Action: A Powerful Historical Response to the Crisis among American Men* (Ben Lomond, Calif.: Conciliar Press, 1996), 15.

19. Christina Hoff Sommers, *The War against Boys* (New York: Simon & Schuster, 2000).

20. Joseph Chilton Pearce, *The Biology of Transcendence: A Blueprint of the Human Spirit* (Rochester, Vt.: Park Street Press, 2002); Paul Pearsall, *The Heart's Code* (New York: Broadway Books, 1998) is saying much the same if you doubt Pearce.

21. Richard Rohr, *Hope against Darkness* (Cincinnati: St. Anthony Messenger Press, 2001), 97–105.

Chapter 3: The Two Births

22. Eckhart Tolle, *The Power of Now* (Novato, Calif.: New World Library, 1999), 29ff.

23. Catholics made one notable exception — Mary did not pass on any original sin to Jesus; she was whole, and we called that the Immaculate Conception. Very few understand and even fewer appreciate this doctrine, although it actually sets the stage for the beauty of Jesus's humanity. Jesus, we said, had a mother who was not wounded ("immaculate" = unstained), which grounded his humanity in calm love and security. In light of what we now know about coparenting, I would argue, with the same logic, for Joseph being "immaculate" too.

Chapter 4: The Big Patterns That Are Always True

24. D. H. Lawrence, "Healing," in *The Complete Poems of D. H. Lawrence,* ed. V. de Sola Pinto and F. W. Roberts (New York: Viking Press, 1971).

25. Joseph Campbell, *The Hero with a Thousand Faces* (Princeton: Bollingen, 1949), 30ff.

Chapter 5: Life Is Hard

26. In the thirteenth century, the issue of "Why the cross?" was already an issue of major debate, and unfortunately the mechanistic juridical answer won the day. Based on many cultic Jewish metaphors of blood, ransom, temple sacrifice, Abraham, and Isaac, the weight of the argument became that God needed the blood of Jesus to pay some kind of cosmic debt. Literal interpretation of spiritual metaphors is always the death of religion; it keeps the real meaning external to the soul, instead of ensuring an internal process. We ended up with a horrible atonement theory that makes God the Father into a petty ogre, who is not organically related to his own creation. God needed to decide to love us, but only if the payment was high enough and the suffering great enough. No wonder we have had so few Christians

who loved and trusted God, and so many who feared and even disliked God. Is this not at the heart of Western atheism? Fortunately, Blessed John Duns Scotus, a Franciscan theologian of the thirteenth century, taught what is now common sense. Jesus was not paying any debt, except possibly to the hardened human psyche. He did not have to die to get God to love us. His death allowed us to love and trust God. He died so we could see in his body what God was like — to understand self-sacrificing love. Jesus was not changing God's mind about us, but changing our mind about God!

27. Eckhart Tolle, *The Power of Now* (Novato, Calif.: New World Library, 1999).

28. Richard Rohr, *Simplicity: The Art of Living,* trans. Peter Heinegg (New York: Crossroad, 1991). Chap. 6 is entirely devoted to this telling story.

29. René Girard, *The Girard Reader,* ed. James Williams (New York: Crossroad, 1996), 97ff.

30. Richard Rohr, *True Self/False Self* (Cincinnati: St. Anthony Messenger, 2002), taped conference.

31. Gerard Manley Hopkins, S.J., "Hurrahing in Harvest," *A Hopkins Reader* (Garden City, N.Y.: Doubleday, 1966), 51.

32. Richard Rohr, *Quest for the Grail* (New York: Crossroad, 1994).

Chapter 6: You Are Not Important

33. Basho Matsuo, *The Narrow Road to the Deep North and Other Travel Sketches* (Baltimore: Penguin Books, 1966), 9.

Chapter 8: You Are Not in Control

34. Gerald May, *Will and Spirit* (San Francisco: Harper & Row, 1982), 6.

35. Rainer Maria Rilke, "The Watcher," translation by Richard Rohr.

36. Ken Wilber, *Sex, Ecology, Spirituality* (Boston: Shambhala, 1995), 22ff.

37. Ibid.,16.

38. Robert Bly, *The Sibling Society* (Amherst, Mass.: Addison-Wesley, 1996).

39. Francis Ianni, *The Search for Structure* (New York: Free Press, 1989); and Wade Clark Roof, *A Generation of Seekers* (San Francisco: HarperSanFrancisco, 1994).

40. Ronald Johnson, *Rites of Passage: Boys and Fatherhood,* C-SPAN 73226, 1996, video.

41. Janet O. Hagberg, *Real Power: Stages of Power in Organizations* (Minneapolis: Winston Press, 1984).

42. Richard Rohr, *Soul Brothers: Men in the Bible Speak to Men Today* (Maryknoll, N.Y.: Orbis, 2004), 53ff.

43. *The Responsibilities of Initiated Men* (Albuquerque, N.Mex.: Center for Action and Contemplation, 2003), video.

44. Erich Fromm, *The Art of Loving* (New York: Harper and Row, 1956), 43ff.

45. Richard Rohr, *The Wild Man's Journey* (Cincinnati: St. Anthony Messenger Press, 1992), 79–90.

46. I suspect this is why we named the Trinity in male terms of Father and Son, although they are just metaphors. But why did Jesus himself choose such metaphors? The male longing is revealed in the words "Father" and "Son," mutually giving and receiving from one another.

47. Rohr, *The Wild Man's Journey*, 187ff.

48. W. B. Yeats, *The Collected Works of W. B. Yeats,* vol. 1: *The Poems, Revised* (New York: Macmillan, 1961).

Chapter 9: You Are Going to Die

49. James Hoopes, ed., *Peirce on Signs: Writings on Semiotics* (Chapel Hill: University of North Carolina Press, 1991), 189.

50. Ernest Becker, *The Denial of Death* (New York: Free Press, 1973), 47.

51. Hoopes, ed., *Peirce on Signs,* 189.

52. Belden Lane, *The Solace of Fierce Landscapes: Exploring Desert and Mountain Spirituality* (New York: Oxford University Press, 1998). An excellent presentation of this theme and many others.

53. D. H. Lawrence, *Studies in Classic American Literature* (New York: T. Seltzer, 1923).

54. Eckhart Tolle, *Stillness Speaks* (Novato, Calif.: New World Library, 2003), 127.

55. *Dei Verbum,* Dogmatic Constitution on Divine Revelation (New York: Guild Press, 1966), 112, #2.

56. Indeed, we might say that most organizations are organized to avoid any disenchantment with themselves and to mystify their own importance. Every wise institution, therefore, is wise precisely

because it allows a loyal opposition and blesses its prophets, inside and out. Otherwise, religion is far too often an inoculation against authentic religious experience. It gives you too much ego and group satisfaction so you can avoid the search for the real thing. After a while it puts most of its energy into self-preservation, self-maintenance, and self-promotion. In such idolatrous worship of forms, words, dates, places, and group symbols, we have laid a foundation for much of the political violence and religious hatred in human history. Whenever you have an overly strong in-group, you will need to define yourself in opposition to out-groups.

Chapter 10: What Is the Shape of the Male Soul?

57. Robert Moore and Douglas Gillette, *King, Warrior, Magician, Lover: Rediscovering the Archetypes of Mature Masculinity* (San Francisco: HarperCollins, 1990).

58. Patrick Arnold, *Wildmen, Warriors, and Kings: Masculine Spirituality and the Bible* (New York: Crossroad, 1991), 180–99.

59. Michael Talbot, *The Holographic Universe* (New York: HarperCollins, 1991), 32ff.

Chapter 11: The Four Initiations

60. Chogyam Trungpa, *Shambhala: The Sacred Path of the Warrior* (Boston: Shambhala, 1984).

61. Robert Moore and Douglas Gillette, *The Magician Within* (New York: Avon Books, 1993).

62. Kenan B. Osborne, *The Franciscan Intellectual Tradition* (St. Bonaventure, N.Y.: St. Bonaventure University, 2003).

63. Robert Moore and Douglas Gillette, *The Lover Within* (New York: William Morrow, 1993).

64. Eugene Kennedy, *The Unhealed Wound: The Church and Human Sexuality* (New York: St. Martin's Griffin, 2001).

65. Alan Watts, *Behold the Spirit* (New York: Random House, 1947). This is one of my top ten books that named my own experience of church and religion.

66. Richard Rohr, *The Great Themes of Paul* (Cincinnati: St. Anthony Messenger Press, 2001), taped set.

67. Robert Moore and Douglas Gillette, *The King Within* (New York: William Morrow, 1992).

Chapter 12: All Transformation Takes Place in Liminal Space

68. Victor Turner, *The Ritual Process* (Ithaca, N.Y.: Cornell University Press, 1969).

69. Ibid., 145ff.

70. Richard Rohr, *The Spirituality of Subtraction* (Cincinnati: St. Anthony Messenger Press), tape set.

71. Richard Rohr, *Beginner's Mind* (Albuquerque, N.Mex.: Center for Action and Contemplation, 2002), tape and CD.

72. Robert Moore, *The Archetype of Initiation* (Philadelphia: Xlibris, 2001), 49ff.

73. Turner, *The Ritual Process*, 145, 151.

Chapter 13: So How Do We Do It?

74. Leon Podles, *The Church Impotent* (Dallas: Spence, 1999), 113ff. The book might make you angry, and you might not agree with everything, but it is hard to dismiss his major thrust and argument.

75. William Loader, *Jesus and the Fundamentalism of His Day* (Grand Rapids, Mich.: Eerdmans, 2001).

76. John Meier, *A Marginal Jew: Rethinking the Historical Jesus* (New York: Doubleday, 2001).

Chapter 14: Jesus's Five Messages

77. Tom Stella, *A Faith Worth Believing* (San Francisco: Harper, 2004).

78. Anne Wilson Schaef, *When Society Becomes an Addict* (New York: Harper & Row, 1987).

79. Richard Rohr, *The Shape of God: Deepening the Mystery of the Trinity* (Albuquerque, N.Mex.: Center for Action and Contemplation, 2004), four CDs.

80. Gerard Manley Hopkins, *A Hopkins Reader* (New York: Doubleday, 1966), 67.

81. Craig Bullock, *The Path to Healing* (Rochester, N.Y.: Assisi Institute, 1999). This book on love is one of the most profound on the subject I have ever read, and for me it is a perfect example of Jesus's words that the student will do much greater things than the teacher. Craig Bullock has been a spiritual son to me for many years.

Appendix

82. Robert Moore, *The Archetype of Initiation* (Philadelphia: Xlibris, 1991), 57, 64, 108ff.

83. Victor Turner, *The Ritual Process* (Ithaca, N.Y.: Cornell University Press, 1969), 103.

84. We still speak of Baptism, Confirmation, and Holy Orders as leaving an indelible mark on the soul. I do not think that one's function in ministry (Holy Orders) is indelible, and the church finally admits as much by permitting laicization. It is a completely different category than the soul's being inherently touched by God. The God encounter that is sacramentalized in Baptism, Confirmation, and Eucharist is a touch of being, not just a call to a role within the community, as Holy Orders is. You can never undo having been touched by God, though you may think you can forget the touch. You can, however, change community roles, and sometimes you should. I firmly believe some people are called to ministry for a while or for a purpose, just as we see in some of the prophets, like Amos and Jonah, and perhaps most of the apostles, since we know absolutely nothing of most of them after the resurrection. Their job was corporate, historical, and probably temporary. God seems to use people for purposes much more than for roles and structured lifestyles.

BIBLIOGRAPHY

Alexander, Marilyn Bennett, and James Preston. *We Were Baptized Too: Claiming God's Grace for Lesbians and Gays.* Louisville: Westminster John Knox, 1996.

Alison, James. *Faith Beyond Resentment.* London: Darton, Longman and Todd, 2001.

———. *The Joy of Being Wrong: Original Sin through Easter Eyes.* New York: Crossroad Herder, 1998.

———. *Raising Abel: The Recovery of the Eschatological Imagination.* New York: Crossroad Herder, 1996.

Anderson, Sherry Ruth, and Patricia Hopkins. *The Feminine Face of God: The Unfolding of the Sacred in Women.* New York: Bantam, 1991.

Arnold, Patrick M. *Wildmen, Warriors, and Kings: Masculine Spirituality and the Bible.* New York: Crossroad, 1991.

Atwater, P. M. H., LhD. *Children of the New Millennium: Children's Near-Death Experiences and the Evolution of Humankind.* New York: Three Rivers Press, 1999.

Bailie, Gil. *Violence Unveiled: Humanity at the Crossroads.* New York: Crossroad, 1995.

Barnhart, Bruno. *Second Simplicity: The Inner Shape of Christianity.* New York and Mahwah, N.J.: Paulist Press, 1999.

Beck, Peggy V., and Anna L. Walters. *The Sacred: Ways of Knowledge, Sources of Life.* Tsaile, Ariz.: Navajo Community College Press, 1977.

Becker, Ernest. *The Denial of Death.* New York: Free Press, 1973.

Berger, Peter L. *A Rumor of Angels: Modern Society and the Rediscovery of the Supernatural.* New York: Anchor Books, 1969.

Berman, Phillip L. *The Journey Home: What Near-Death Experiences and Mysticism Teach Us about the Gift of Life.* New York: Pocket Books, 1996.

Bly, Robert. *Iron John: A Book about Men.* New York: Addison-Wesley, 1990.

———. *The Sibling Society.* New York: Addison-Wesley, 1996.

Boff, Leonardo. *Holy Trinity: Perfect Community.* Maryknoll, N.Y.: Orbis, 1988.

Borgman, Albert. *Crossing the Postmodern Divide.* Chicago: University of Chicago Press, 1992.

Bourgeault, Cynthia. *Mystical Hope: Trusting in the Mercy of God.* Boston: Cowley, 2001.

——. *The Wisdom Way of Knowing.* San Francisco: Jossey-Bass, 2003.

Boyd, Stephen B. W., Merle Longwood, and Mark W. Muesse, eds. *Redeeming Men: Religion and Masculinities.* Louisville: Westminster John Knox, 1996.

Brewi, Janice, and Anne Brennan. *Celebrate Mid-Life: Jungian Archetypes and Mid-Life Spirituality.* New York: Crossroad, 1988.

Brueggemann, Walter. *The Prophetic Imagination.* Philadelphia: Fortress Press, 1978.

Buber, Martin. *I and Thou.* 2nd ed. New York: Charles Scribner's Sons, 1958.

Bullock, Craig. *The Path to Healing: Experiencing God as Love.* Rochester, N.Y.: Assisi Institute, 1999.

Campbell, Joseph. *The Hero with a Thousand Faces.* Princeton, N.J.: Princeton University Press, 1949.

——. *Thou Art That: Transforming Religious Metaphor.* Novato, Calif.: New World Library, 2001.

Caprio, Betsy. *The Woman Sealed in the Tower: A Psychological Approach to Feminine Spirituality.* New York and Ramsey, N.J.: Paulist Press, 1982.

Carotenuto, Aldo. *The Vertical Labyrinth: Individuation in Jungian Psychology.* Toronto: Inner City Books, 1985.

Chinen, Allan B., M.D. *Beyond the Hero: Classic Stories of Men in Search of Soul.* New York: Tarcher/Putnam, 1993.

Chomsky, Noam. *On Power and Ideology.* New York: Black Rose Books, 1987.

Conner, Randy P. *Blossom of Bone: Reclaiming the Connections between Homoeroticism and the Sacred.* San Francisco: HarperSanFrancisco, 1993.

Cousineau, Phil, ed. *The Hero's Journey: Joseph Campbell on His Life and Work.* San Francisco: HarperSanFrancisco, 1990.

Cousins, Ewert H. *Christ of the 21st Century.* Rockport, Mass.: Element, 1992.

Culbertson, Philip L., ed. *The Spirituality of Men: Sixteen Christians Write about Their Faith.* Minneapolis: Fortress Press, 2002.

de Castillejo, Irene Claremont. *Knowing Woman: A Feminine Psychology.* New York: Harper Colophon Books, 1974.

Downey, Michael. *Digging Deep: Fostering the Spirituality of Young Men.* Winona, Minn.: St. Mary's Press, 2003.

Doyle, James A. *The Male Experience.* Dubuque, Iowa: Wm. C. Brown, 1983.

Dwinell, Michael. *Being Priest to One Another.* Liguori, Mo.: Triumph Books, 1993.

Edinger, Edward. *Ego and Archetype.* New York: Penguin, 1973.

Edwards, Tilden. *Spiritual Director, Spiritual Companion: Guide to Tending the Soul.* New York and Mahwah, N.J.: Paulist Press, 2001.

Eisler, Riane. *The Chalice and the Blade: Our History, Our Future.* San Francisco: Harper & Row, 1987.

Eliade, Mircea. *Myth and Reality.* New York: Harper & Row, 1963.

———. *The Quest: History and Meaning in Religion.* Chicago: University of Chicago Press, 1969.

———. *Rites and Symbols of Initiation: The Mysteries of Birth and Rebirth.* New York: Harper Torchbooks, 1958.

———. *The Sacred and the Profane: The Nature of Religion.* New York: Harcourt, 1957.

———. *Symbolism, the Sacred, and the Arts.* Edited by Diane Apostolos-Cappadona. New York: Crossroad, 1988.

Estés, Clarissa Pinkola, PhD. *Women Who Run with the Wolves: Myths and Stories of the Wild Woman Archetype.* New York: Ballantine Books, 1992.

Field, Anne, O.S.B. *From Darkness to Light: What it Meant to Become a Christian in the Early Church.* Ann Arbor, Mich.: Servant Books, 1978.

Finley, James. *Merton's Palace of Nowhere: A Search for God through Awareness of the True Self.* Notre Dame, Ind.: Ave Maria Press, 1978.

Fiorenza, Elisabeth Schüssler. *Bread Not Stone: The Challenge of Feminist Biblical Interpretation.* Boston: Beacon Press, 1984.

Frankl, Victor E. *Man's Search for Meaning.* New York: Washington Square Press, 1959.

Fromm, Erich. *The Art of Loving.* London: Unwin Paperbacks, 1957.

———. *Escape from Freedom.* New York: Holt, Rinehart, and Winston, 1941.

Fuller, Andrew Reid. *Psychology and Religion: Eight Points of View.* Lanham, Md.: Littlefield Adams, 1994.

Gabriele, Edward Francis. *From Many, One: Praying Our Rich and Diverse Cultural Heritage.* Notre Dame, Ind.: Ave Maria Press, 1995.

Gilmore, David D. *Manhood in the Making: Cultural Concepts of Masculinity.* New Haven: Yale University Press, 1990.

Girard, René. *Violence and the Sacred.* Baltimore: Johns Hopkins University Press, 1972.

Goldberg, Herb, PhD. *The Hazards of Being Male: Surviving the Myth of Masculine Privilege.* New York: Signet, 1976.

Golden, Thomas R. *Swallowed by a Snake: The Gift of the Masculine Side of Healing.* Gaithersburg, Md.: Golden Healing Publishing, 1996.

Goleman, Daniel. *Emotional Intelligence: Why It Can Matter More Than IQ.* New York: Bantam Books, 1995.

Gollaher, David L. *Circumcision: A History of the World's Most Controversial Surgery.* New York: Basic Books, 2000.

Grimes, Ronald L. *Deeply into the Bone: Re-inventing Rites of Passage.* Berkeley: University of California Press, 2000.

Gurian, Michael. *A Fine Young Man: What Parents, Mentors, and Educators Can Do to Shape Adolescent Boys into Exceptional Men.* New York: Tarcher/Putnam, 1998.

———. *The Prince and the King: Healing the Father-Son Wound, A Guided Journey of Initiation.* New York: Tarcher/Perigee, 1992.

Hafiz. *The Gift: Poems by Hafiz, the Great Sufi Master.* Trans. Daniel Ladinsky. New York: Penguin/Arkana, 1999.

Halligan, Fredrica R., and John J. Shea, eds. *The Fires of Desire: Erotic Energies and the Spiritual Quest.* New York: Crossroad, 1992.

Hamerton-Kelly, Robert G. *The Gospel and the Sacred: Poetics of Violence in Mark.* Minneapolis: Fortress Press, 1994.

———. *Sacred Violence: Paul's Hermeneutic of the Cross.* Minneapolis: Fortress Press, 1992.

Hart, Thomas. *What Does It Mean to Be a Man?* New York: Paulist Press, 2004.

Hauerwas, Stanley. *A Community of Character: Toward a Constructive Christian Social Ethic.* Notre Dame, Ind.: University of Notre Dame Press, 1981.

Haughton, Rosemary. *The Transformation of Man: A Study of Conversion and Community.* Springfield, Ill.: Templegate Publishers, 1967.

Herdt, Gilbert H. *Rituals of Manhood: Male Initiation in Papua New Guinea.* Berkeley: University of California Press, 1982.

Heyward, Carter. *Saving Jesus from Those Who Are Right: Rethinking What It Means to Be Christian.* Minneapolis: Fortress Press, 1999.

———. *Speaking of Christ: A Lesbian Feminist Voice.* Ed. Ellen C. Davis. New York: Pilgrim Press, 1989.

———. *Touching Our Strength: The Erotic as Power and the Love of God.* San Francisco: HarperSanFrancisco, 1984.

Hillman, James, Henry A. Murray, Tom Moore, James Baird, Thomas Cowan, and Randolph Severson. *Puer Papers.* Irving, Tex.: Spring Publications, 1979.

Hofer, Markus. *Francis for Men: Otherwise, We Need Weapons.* Cincinnati: St. Anthony Messenger Press, 2001.

Hollis, James. *Under Saturn's Shadow: The Wounding and Healing of Men.* Toronto: Inner City Books, 1994.

Houston, Jean. *The Hero and the Goddess: The Odyssey as Mystery and Initiation.* New York: Ballantine Books, 1992.

———. *The Search for the Beloved: Journeys in Sacred Psychology.* Los Angeles: Tarcher, 1987.

Hunter, James Davidson. *The Death of Character: Moral Education in an Age without Good or Evil.* New York: Basic Books, 2000.

Inchausti, Robert. *The Ignorant Perfection of Ordinary People.* Albany: State University of New York Press, 1991.

James, David C. *What Are They Saying about Masculine Spirituality?* New York and Mahwah, N.J.: Paulist Press, 1996.

———. *Sacred Vision: A Man's Legacy.* San Jose, Calif.: Author's Choice, 2000.

James, William. *The Varieties of Religious Experience: A Study in Human Nature.* New York: Modern Library, 1994.

Janeway, Elizabeth. *Powers of the Weak.* New York: Morrow Quill Paperbacks, 1980.

Johnson, Elizabeth. *She Who Is: The Mystery of God in Feminist Theological Discourse.* New York: Crossroad, 1993.

Johnson, Robert A. *Femininity Lost and Regained.* New York: Harper & Row, 1990.

———. *The Fisher King and the Handless Maiden: Understanding the Wounded Feeling Function in Masculine and Feminine Psychology.* San Francisco: HarperSanFrancisco, 1993.

———. *Transformation: Understanding the Three Levels of Masculine Consciousness.* New York: HarperCollins, 1991.

Jones, Terry. *The Elder Within: The Source of Mature Masculinity.* Wilsonville, Ore.: Book Partners, 2001.

Judy, Dwight H. *Healing the Male Soul: Christianity and the Mythic Journey.* New York: Crossroad, 1992.

Jung, C. G. *Aspects of the Feminine*. Princeton, N.J.: Princeton University Press, 1982.

——. *Aspects of the Masculine*. Princeton, N.J.: Princeton University Press, 1989.

——. *Psychological Reflections*. Princeton, N.J.: Princeton University Press, 1953.

Kabir. *The Kabir Book: Forty-Four of the Ecstatic Poems of Kabir*. Versions by Robert Bly. Boston: Beacon, 1971.

Kauth, Bill. *A Circle of Men: The Original Manual for Men's Support Groups*. New York: St. Martin's Press, 1992.

Keen, Sam. *Fire in the Belly: On Being a Man*. New York: Bantam, 1991.

——. *To a Dancing God: Notes of a Spiritual Traveler*. San Francisco: HarperSanFrancisco, 1990.

Kelsey, Morton. *Myth, History, and Faith: The Mysteries of Christian Myth and Imagination*. Rockport, Mass.: Element, 1974.

——. *Sacrament of Sexuality*. Warwick, N.Y.: Amity, 1986.

Kennedy, Eugene. *The Unhealed Wound: The Church and Human Sexuality*. New York: St. Martin's Griffin, 2001.

Kindlon, Dan, and Michael Thompson. *Raising Cain: Protecting the Emotional Life of Boys*. New York: Ballantine Books, 1999.

Kipnis, Aaron R. *Knights without Armor: A Practical Guide for Men in Quest of Masculine Soul*. New York: Tarcher/Perigee, 1991.

La Cerva, Victor. *Pathways to Peace: Forty Steps to a Less Violent America*. Memphis: Heal Foundation Press, 1996.

Lasch, Christopher. *The Culture of Narcissism: American Life in an Age of Diminishing Expectations*. New York: W. W. Norton, 1979.

Levinson, Daniel. *The Seasons of a Man's Life*. New York: Knopf, 1978.

Lewis, C. S. *The Four Loves*. New York: Harcourt Brace Jovanovich, 1960.

Linn, Denise. *Quest: A Guide for Creating Your Own Vision Quest*. New York: Ballantine Books, 1997.

Lundin, Roger. *The Culture of Interpretation: Christian Faith and the Postmodern World*. Grand Rapids, Mich.: Eerdmans, 1993.

Maalouf, Amin. *In the Name of Identity: Violence and the Need to Belong*. New York: Arcade Publishing, 1996.

Madden, Lawrence, ed. *The Joseph Campbell Phenomenon: Implications for the Contemporary Church*. Washington, D.C.: Pastoral Press, 1992.

Mahdi, Louise Carus, Nancy Geyer Christopher, and Michael Meade, eds. *Crossroads: The Quest for Contemporary Rites of Passage.* Chicago: Open Court, 1996.

Mahdi, Louise Carus, Steven Foster, and Meredith Little, eds. *Betwixt and Between: Patterns of Masculine and Feminine Initiation.* La Salle, Ill.: Open Court, 1987.

Malina, Bruce J., and Richard L. Rohrbaugh. *Social-Science Commentary on the Synoptic Gospels.* Minneapolis: Fortress Press, 1992.

Maslow, A. H. *Religions, Values, and Peak Experiences.* New York: Penguin, 1964.

May, Gerald G., M.D. *Addiction and Grace.* San Francisco: Harper & Row, 1988.

———. *The Dark Night of the Soul:* San Francisco: Harper & Row, 2004.

May, Rollo. *The Cry for Myth.* New York: Delta, 1991.

McCarthy, Cormac. *All the Pretty Horses.* New York: Vintage Books, 1992.

Meier, John P. *A Marginal Jew: Rethinking the Historical Jesus.* New York: Doubleday, 2001.

Miedzian, Myriam. *Boys Will Be Boys: Breaking the Link Between Masculinity and Violence.* New York: Doubleday, 1991.

Miller, Robert J. *Grief Quest: Reflections for Men Coping with Loss.* St. Meinrad, Ind.: Abbey Press, 1996.

Miller, William A. *Make Friends with Your Shadow: How to Accept and Use Positively the Negative Side of Your Personality.* Minneapolis: Augsburg Publishing House, 1981.

Miller, William R., and Janet C'de Baca. *Quantum Change: When Epiphanies and Sudden Insights Transform Ordinary Lives.* New York: Guilford Press, 2001.

Mitscherlich, Alexander. *Society without the Father: A Contribution to Social Psychology.* New York: HarperPerennial, 1963.

Monette, Paul. *Becoming a Man: Half a Life Story.* New York: Harcourt Brace Jovanovich, 1992.

Monick, Eugene. *Phallos: Sacred Image of the Masculine.* Toronto: Inner City Books, 1987.

Moore, Robert L. *The Archetype of Initiation: Sacred Space, Ritual Process, and Personal Transformation.* Philadelphia: Xlibris, 2001.

———. *Facing the Dragon: Confronting Personal and Spiritual Grandiosity.* Ed. Max J. Havlick Jr. Wilmette, Ill.: Chiron Publications, 2003.

Moore, Robert, and Douglas Gillette. *The Lover Within: Accessing the Lover in the Male Psyche.* New York: William Morrow, 1993.

———. *The Magician Within: Accessing the Shaman in the Male Psyche.* New York: Avon Books, 1993.

———. *The Warrior Within: Accessing the Knight in the Male Psyche.* New York: William Morrow, 1992.

Murphy Center for Liturgical Research. *Made, Not Born: New Perspectives on Christian Initiation and the Catechumenate.* Notre Dame, Ind.: University of Notre Dame Press, 1976.

Myers, Ched. *Binding the Strong Man: A Political Reading of Mark's Story of Jesus.* Maryknoll, N.Y.: Orbis, 1988.

Myers, Ched, Marie Dennis, Joseph Nangle, O.F.M., Cynthia Moe-Lobeda, and Stuart Taylor. *"Say to This Mountain": Mark's Story of Discipleship.* Maryknoll, N.Y.: Orbis, 1997.

Naranjo, Claudio. *The Divine Child and the Hero: Inner Meaning in Children's Literature.* Nevada City, Calif.: Gateways, 1999.

Nelson, James B. *The Intimate Connection: Male Sexuality, Masculine Spirituality.* Philadelphia: Westminster Press, 1988.

Nelson, James B., and Sandra P. Longfellow, eds. *Sexuality and the Sacred: Sources for Theological Reflection.* Louisville: Westminster John Knox, 1994.

Nouwen, Henri. *The Return of the Prodigal Son.* New York: Doubleday, 1994.

Oliva, Max. *The Masculine Spirit: Resources for Reflective Living.* Notre Dame, Ind.: Ave Maria Press, 1997.

Osborne, Kenan B., O.F.M. *The Christian Sacraments of Initiation: Baptism, Confirmation, Eucharist.* New York and Mahwah, N.J.: Paulist Press, 1987.

Pable, Martin W., O.F.M. *A Man and His God: Contemporary Male Spirituality.* Notre Dame, Ind.: Ave Maria Press, 1988.

———. *The Quest for the Male Soul: In Search of Something More.* Notre Dame, Ind.: Ave Maria Press, 1996.

Paladin, Lynda S. *Ceremonies for Change: Creating Rituals to Heal Life's Hurts.* Walpole, N.H.: Stillpoint, 1991.

Papesh, Michael. *Clerical Culture: Contradiction and Transformation.* Collegeville, Minn.: Liturgical Press, 2004.

Pearson, Carol S. *Awakening the Heroes Within: Twelve Archetypes to Help Us Find Ourselves and Transform Our World.* San Francisco: HarperSanFrancisco, 1991.

——. *The Hero Within: Six Archetypes We Live By.* San Francisco: HarperSanFrancisco, 1986.

Peck, M. Scott. *People of the Lie: The Hope for Healing Human Evil.* New York: Simon and Schuster, 1983.

Pieper, Josef. *The Silence of St. Thomas.* South Bend, Ind.: St. Augustine's Press, 1999.

Podles, Leon J. *The Church Impotent: The Feminization of Christianity.* Dallas: Spence, 1999.

Rahner, Karl. *The Shape of the Church to Come.* New York: Seabury Press, 1972.

Rambuss, Richard. *Closet Devotions.* Durham, N.C.: Duke University Press, 1998.

Rappaport, Roy A. *Ritual and Religion in the Making of Humanity.* Cambridge: Cambridge University Press, 1999.

Rieff, Philip. *The Triumph of the Therapeutic: Uses of Faith after Freud.* Chicago: University of Chicago Press, 1966.

Rohr, Richard. "Beyond Crime and Punishment." *Sojourners* 31, no. 4 (July–August 2002): 26–29, 59.

——. "Boys to Men: Rediscovering Rites of Passage for Our Time." *Sojourners* 27, no. 3 (May–June 1998): 16–21.

——. *Called, Formed, Sent.* With Thomas C. Welch. Rockford, Ill.: National Association of Diaconate Directors, 2002.

——. *Everything Belongs.* New York: Crossroad, 1999.

——. "Grieving as Sacred Space." *Sojourners* 31, no. 1 (January–February 2002): 20–24.

——. *Hope against Darkness.* Cincinnati: St. Anthony Messenger Press, 2001.

——. *Quest for the Grail.* New York: Crossroad, 1999.

——. *Soul Brothers: Men in the Bible Speak to Men Today.* Maryknoll, N.Y.: Orbis, 2004.

——. *The Wild Man's Journey: Reflections on Male Spirituality.* Cincinnati: St. Anthony Messenger Press, 1992.

Roof, Wade Clark. *A Generation of Seekers: The Spiritual Journeys of the Baby Boom Generation.* San Francisco: HarperSanFrancisco, 1993.

Ross, Maggie. *The Fountain and the Furnace: The Way of Tears and Fire.* New York: Paulist Press, 1987.

Rumi. *The Soul of Rumi: A New Collection of Ecstatic Poems.* Trans. Coleman Barks. San Francisco: HarperSanFrancisco, 2001.

Schaffran, Janet, and Pat Kozak. *More Than Words: Prayer and Ritual for Inclusive Communities.* New York: Crossroad, 1986.

Shenitz, Bruce, ed. *The Man I Might Become: Gay Men Write about Their Fathers.* New York: Marlowe, 2002.

Simmons, Philip. *Learning to Fall: The Blessings of an Imperfect Life.* New York: Bantam, 2000.

Smith, Huston. *Beyond the Post-Modern Mind.* Updated and revised. Wheaton, Ill.: Theosophical Publishing House, 1982.

———. *Forgotten Truth: The Common Vision of the World's Religions.* San Francisco: HarperSanFrancisco, 1976.

———. *Why Religion Matters: The Fate of the Human Spirit in an Age of Disbelief.* San Francisco: HarperSanFrancisco, 2001.

Sommers, Christina Hoff. *The War against Boys: How Misguided Feminism Is Harming Our Young Men.* New York: Touchstone, 2000.

Stein, Murray. *In MidLife: A Jungian Perspective.* Dallas, Tex.: Spring Publications, 1983.

Strage, Mark. *The Durable Fig Leaf.* New York: Dorset, 1980.

Sullivan, Andrew. *Love Undetectable: Notes on Friendship, Sex, and Survival.* New York: Vintage Books, 1998.

Sussman, Linda. *The Speech of the Grail: A Journey toward Speaking That Heals and Transforms.* Hudson, N.Y.: Lindisfarne Press, 1995.

Tacey, David J. *Edge of the Sacred: Transformation in Australia.* Victoria, Australia: HarperCollins, 1995.

———. *Remaking Men: The Revolution in Masculinity.* Victoria, Australia: Viking, 1997.

Tagore, Rabindranath. *Gitanjali.* Bandra, Mumbai: Better Yourself Books, 2001.

Tarnas, Richard. *The Passion of the Western Mind: Understanding the Ideas That Have Shaped Our World View.* New York: Ballantine Books, 1991.

Teilhard de Chardin, Pierre. *The Phenomenon of Man.* New York: Harper, 1955.

Thompson, Keith, ed. *To Be a Man: In Search of the Deep Masculine.* Los Angeles: Tarcher, 1991.

Tillich, Paul. *The Courage to Be.* London: Collins, 1952.

Tolle, Eckhart. *The Power of Now: A Guide to Spiritual Enlightenment.* Novato, Calif.: New World Library, 1999.

Trungpa, Chögyam. *Cutting Through Spiritual Materialism.* Boston: Shambhala, 1987.

———. *The Sacred Path of the Warrior.* Boston: Shambhala, 1984.

Tugwell, Simon, O.P. *Ways of Imperfection: An Exploration of Christian Spirituality.* London: Darton, Longman, and Todd, 1984.

Turner, Victor. *The Ritual Process: Structure and Anti-Structure.* Ithaca, N.Y.: Cornell University Press, 1969.

Ulanov, Ann Belford. *The Wisdom of the Psyche.* Cambridge, Mass.: Cowley Publications, 1988.

Van Gennep, Arnold. *The Rites of Passage.* Chicago: University of Chicago Press, 1960.

Vitz, Paul C. *Psychology as Religion: The Cult of Self-Worship.* Grand Rapids, Mich.: Eerdmans, 1977.

Watts, Alan W. *Behold the Spirit.* New York: Random House, 1947.

———. *The Wisdom of Insecurity: A Message for an Age of Anxiety.* New York: Vintage Books, 1951.

Weaver, Mary Jo, and R. Scott Appleby. *Being Right: Conservative Catholics in America.* Bloomington: Indiana University Press, 1995.

Welch, John. *Spiritual Pilgrims: Carl Jung and Teresa of Avila.* New York: Paulist Press, 1982.

West, Cornel. *Prophetic Thought in Postmodern Times.* Monroe, Maine: Common Courage Press, 1993.

Wilber, Ken. *A Brief History of Everything.* Boston: Shambhala, 1996.

———. *The Essential Ken Wilber: An Introductory Reader.* Boston: Shambhala, 1998.

———. *Sex, Ecology, Spirituality.* Boston: Shambhala, 1995.

Wilber, Ken, Jack Engler, and Daniel P. Brown. *Transformations of Consciousness: Conventional and Contemplative Perspectives on Development.* Boston: New Science Library, 1986.

Williams, Rowan. *Christ on Trial: How the Gospel Unsettles our Judgment.* London: Harper Collins, 2000.

———. *The Wound of Knowledge.* Boston: Cowley, 1979.

Wostyn, Lode L. *A New Church for a New Age.* Quezon City, Philippines: Claretian Publications, 1997.

Wyly, James. *The Phallic Quest: Priapus and Masculine Inflation.* Toronto: Inner City Books, 1989.

Xavier, N. S. *The Two Faces of Religion: A Psychiatrist's View.* Tuscaloosa, Ala.: Portals Press, 1987.

Yarnold, Edward, S.J. *The Awe-Inspiring Rites of Initiation: The Origins of the R.C.I.A.* Collegeville, Minn.: Liturgical Press, 1971.

Zimmer, Heinrich. *Myths and Symbols in Indian Art and Civilization.* New York: Harper & Row, 1946.

ACKNOWLEDGMENTS

There were many steps, many stages, and many friends and connections that led me to write this book. I would like to acknowledge and thank as many as possible. Please forgive me if you appear forgotten. "Your names are written in heaven!"

I must begin with my own dear father, Richard Rohr Sr., who gave me the foundational experience of very good fatherhood and quiet initiation. The Franciscans of the Cincinnati Province educated me formally for thirteen years and gave me my initiating "novitiate" under dear Fr. Benno Heidlage, O.F.M., who was a man in every good sense, then especially Fr. Paul Desch, O.F.M., Fr. Leander Blumlein, O.F.M., Fr. Larry Landini, O.F.M, and Cyrin Maus, who freed me to think creatively, but with the philosophical and theological grounding in the perennial tradition.

Once I became a "father" myself it was largely the "sons" and "daughters" who taught me, especially the young people of the New Jerusalem Community in Cincinnati, where I was the founder and pastor for fourteen years. I dare not mention one name or hundreds will feel forgotten. You know who you are, and you know how you grew me up! Thank you, because it is my spiritual "children" who have called forth my fatherhood.

Intellectually, it was the writings of Robert Bly, Robert Moore, Victor Turner, Mircea Eliade, Joseph Campbell, and the study of the classic Quest for the Holy Grail tradition that most convinced me I was not crazy in thinking this way. I want to thank Stephen Gambill, who was my partner in giving the first Rites of Passage at Ghost Ranch in New Mexico, and Stephen Picha, the director of the Center for Action and Contemplation, who has backed me up and encouraged me in this work like no one else.

Personally, it was often wonderful and painful conversations with father figures, brother partners, and loving sons that brought these ideas to the level of passion and conviction. They know who they are, and they know how I love them. I want especially to mention the fourteen years of jail chaplaincy in Albuquerque, which led me into concrete encounters with thousands of wounded men who always had one thing in common—a not very good father. The poor men of numerous underdeveloped countries taught me by the humble way they carried their wounds, the vigor of their manhood, and how eagerly they still wanted to be fathered.

Practically, I want to thank Joseph Martos, a first-rate sacramental theologian, who made my original thoughts on male spirituality into *The Wild Man's Journey* in 1991, and Michael J. Farrell, who did the same with the *Quest for the Grail* in 1994. Finally I am so grateful to Roy M. Carlisle and John Jones at the Crossroad Publishing Company, and Robert H. Hopcke, who all took a personal interest in this book, and patiently worked with my meandering writing style and my eccentric flights into enthusiasm, diversion, criticism, and saying way too much!

I am a grateful son to all the above "fathers."

ABOUT THE AUTHOR

Richard Rohr, O.F.M., is a Franciscan priest of the New Mexico Province. He was the founder of the New Jerusalem Community in Cincinnati, Ohio, in 1971, and, in 1986, the Center for Action and Contemplation in Albuquerque, New Mexico, where he presently serves as Founding Director. The Center is intended to serve a dual purpose, not only as a radical voice for peaceful, nonviolent social change but also as a forum for renewal and encouragement for the individual who seeks direction from and understanding of God's will and love. Richard was born in 1943 in Kansas. He entered the Franciscans in 1961 and was ordained to the priesthood in 1970. He received his master's degree in theology from Dayton that same year. He now lives in a hermitage behind his Franciscan community in Albuquerque and divides his time between local work and preaching and teaching on all continents. He is well known for his numerous audio and videotapes and for his articles in the Center's newsletter, *Radical Grace.* He is a regular contributing editor/writer for *Sojourners* magazine and recently published a seven-part Lenten series for the *National Catholic Reporter.* He has a best-selling tape series called *The NEW Great Themes of Scripture.* Fr. Rohr has authored books in the areas of male spirituality, the use of the Enneagram in spiritual direction, Scripture, spirituality, and contemplative prayer.

Index

Of Related Interest
by Paula D'Arcy

SACRED THRESHOLD
Crossing the Inner Barrier to a Deeper Love

Includes the author's own story of her relationship with Morrie Schwartz of *Tuesdays with Morrie* and other stories of healing and love

Something new and unanticipated happened when I read Paula's new book, *Sacred Threshold*. She not only brought me to the threshold with which I separate myself from God, she opened me up to the startling discovery of who I am. This book is a must-read for all who want to know the Genuine.

–Rev. John Blackwell, Ph.D.,
author of *Noonday Demon*

0-8245-2278-8, $17.95 hardcover

SEEKING WITH ALL MY HEART
Encountering God's Presence Today

With her distinctive literary style and spiritual insights, Paula D'Arcy brings fresh air to our spiritual reading. Here, in short, meditative essays, she reflects on twenty-nine passages from Scripture and shows how they are powerful, unpredictable, and life-giving.

0-8245-2109-9, $19.95 hardcover

crossroad

Of Related Interest
by Paula D'Arcy

THE GIFT OF THE RED BIRD
A Spiritual Encounter

"To say that *The Gift of the Red Bird* moved me deeply seems inadequate. I wept for its beauty, pain, and joy. It is a powerful testimony to how the Divine woos the soul into a sacred embrace. Paula D'Arcy's vulnerability and courage in narrating her true story of this Divine encounter are remarkable." — Joyce Rupp

0-8245-1956-6, $14.95 paperback

A NEW SET OF EYES
Encountering the Hidden God

Through a series of meditations and parables, D'Arcy helps readers awaken the mind to the presence of God, free the soul from its cherished idols, and infuse the emotions with joy. By the popular author of *Gift of the Red Bird* and *Song for Sarah*.

0-8245-1930-2, $16.95 hardcover

crossroad

Also by Richard Rohr

EVERYTHING BELONGS
The Gift of Contemplative Prayer

Revised & Updated!

Richard Rohr has written this book to help us pray better and see life differently. Using parables, koans, and personal experiences, he leads us beyond the techniques of prayer to a place where we can receive the gift of contemplation: the place where (if only for a moment) we see the world in God clearly, and know that everything belongs.

"Rohr at his finest: insightful cultural critique — with strong connection to the marginalized."
— *The Other Side*

A personal retreat for those who hunger for a deeper prayer life but don't know what contemplation really is or how to let it happen.

0-8245-1995-7, $16.95 paperback

crossroad

Also by Richard Rohr

JOB AND THE MYSTERY OF SUFFERING
Spiritual Reflections

"The author's spiritual reflections on Job are invigorating and wide-reaching. Rohr comments on the nature of evil, the vocation of being a bridge-builder, the way questions unfold the soul, the church of the future, and the role of the poor in it."

—*Values and Vision*

0-8245-1734-2, $18.95 paperback

THE GOOD NEWS ACCORDING TO LUKE
Spiritual Reflections

Now in Paperback!

Grounded in scholarship but accessible to a general audience, this spiritual commentary sheds light on the main themes of Luke's Gospel. Rohr addresses individual concerns, duties, and possibilities, and then connects them to the larger picture of cultural and ecclesial postures, emphases, and values.

"Rohr not only offers a wealth of insight on Luke, but also proclaims a clarion call for us to follow Jesus today."   —*Spiritual Book News*

0-8245-1966-3, $16.95 paperback

crossroad

Also by Richard Rohr

SIMPLICITY
The Art of Living

"Rohr's kind of contemplation is an adventure in the wilderness, letting God call me by name and take me to a deeper place of the peace that the world cannot give and can no longer take from one once it is encountered." —*St. Anthony Messenger*

0-8245-2115-3, $17.95, paperback

QUEST FOR THE GRAIL

Winner of the Catholic Book Award (1995)

"This is a great book for those interested in masculine spirituality since Richard speaks from his experience—the spiritual guide sharing his journey."

—*Praying*

0-8245-1654-0, $19.95 paperback

Please support your local bookstore,
or call 1-800-707-0670 for Customer Service.

For a free catalog, write us at

THE CROSSROAD PUBLISHING COMPANY
16 Penn Plaza, 481 Eighth Avenue
New York, NY 10001

Visit our website at
www.crossroadpublishing.com
All prices subject to change.

crossroad